Debi & Andy,

Enjoy!

THE
SLEEP-WELL-AT-NIGHT
INVESTOR

*Financial Truths that Wall Street
Hopes You Never Discover*

Tim Decker

NORTH AMERICA PRESS

ST. PETERSBURG   MONTREAL

Published in the United States by North America Press, Inc., St. Petersburg, and simultaneously in Canada by North America Press of Canada Limited, Montreal.

ISBN 978-1-60530-047-4

Cover design and charts by Bruno Le Lann

Text layout by North America Press, Inc.

The dissemination of this material is not meant to provide specific financial advice for anyone. Nor does it constitute a recommendation, solicitation, or offer of the purchase or sale of securities. The material contained in this book is meant to provide information not easily found elsewhere and is intended to help investors formulate their financial opinions in a more objective light.

With any investment or investment strategy, outcomes depend on many factors, including: investment objectives, income, net worth, tax bracket, risk tolerance, as well as economic and market factors.

Past performance of any investment vehicle is not an indicator of future performance. Before investing or using any investment strategy, individuals should consult with their tax, legal, or investment adviser.

THE
SLEEP-WELL-AT-NIGHT
INVESTOR

*Financial Truths that Wall Street
Hopes You Never Discover*

Tim Decker

Contents

Contents

Foreword

I learned at an early age from my mother and father how important it was to develop a hard work ethic if I ever wanted to "get ahead." In fact, during most summers all through junior high and senior high school, while most of my friends would just relax (swim, hunt, fish, etc.), my father and I would often begin working as early as 6 in the morning.

My father was a schoolteacher, so during his summers off he would build houses, remodel, paint and so on. Although he might give me a day off now and then, most often I was expected to get up early to help him. And, in spite of the fact that I often complained and wished I too could hang out with my friends, I did learn firsthand many skills and, most importantly, the life lesson that a good, hard work ethic can lead to many great opportunities – that if you don't want to accept mediocrity as a way of life, you don't have to.

In addition, I have been athletic and actively involved in sports while in high school and college and now as a coach. So, suffice it to say I am as competitive a person as you'll ever meet. If I'm going to compete, I always prefer to win. Unfortunately, I don't always get what I prefer, but learning how to handle a defeat with class takes discipline. Fortunately, I have learned over the years how important this is, and now as a coach I always instill this in my players.

So, when entering the financial services profession in 1984, I was excited and enthusiastic about the possibilities awaiting me. I just knew that if I worked harder than most, cared more about my clients than other financial advisers, and was willing to put more hours into researching investment opportunities than others would, I could help my clients achieve "above average" results. Surely this would happen (so I believed), because as I had learned from my earlier years that working hard and being willing to practice harder than most usually led to outstanding results.

Well, after about 17 years of believing this and applying this approach on behalf of all my clients, I became more and more frustrated and at times discouraged. After hours upon hours of research, looking for the "best" for my clients, why did it always seem that the investment strategies and vehicles I would implement would most often under-perform the "boring," no-research required, index funds? How could this be?

When I looked into this question further, I discovered that most of the largest and respected money managers on Wall Street didn't even beat the simple indexes. It was this discovery that led me to step back, choose to have an open mind, and begin researching what Nobel Laureates in financial academia had been writing about for years – writings and lessons that Wall Street hoped most investors would never discover and implement.

That's why I've written this book. I want you also to learn what I discovered and now utilize not only for my clients, but for myself as well. Most of what you will read is not my original thinking. I believe that truth is never invented, just discovered. I hope to educate you and personally challenge you to take a step back, be honest with yourself, and then take the necessary steps that can significantly improve your own probabilities of achieving financial freedom.

There are no shortcuts, no secret formulas, as you will read. But, as I always tell my clients, I have an obligation both legally and morally to tell you what I believe is in your best interest and not what you may always want to hear. It is that promise I make to you as you read this book. Your role is only to have an open mind. You may learn some things that can literally change your financial life. And, if you're so inclined, I would love to hear from you about how this book has had an impact on you.

I would like to thank the following for all of their support and encouragement as I took on the challenge of writing this book. First, all of my clients across the country and overseas who not only are why we come to work every day but also the many who have become very special friends. Nothing means more to me (and my staff) than knowing what we do for you allows you to enjoy your life without losing any sleep worrying about your financial security. I'd also like to thank my world-class staff who provide service that is second to none, and whose efforts consistently provide our clients with the positive experience they deserve. Without them, ISI Financial Group wouldn't exist.

Lastly, I wish to honor my two awesome and special kids – Amanda & Garit, and finally Keith & Velda Decker, my parents. I thank God for the privilege of being your son and I count my blessings often. I only hope that you can, in some small way, see in me what you worked so tirelessly to give.

Wall Street Seducers

Feeding Egos, Egging On Vices & Making a Killing

"This message – that you should not try to beat the market – can never be sold on Wall Street, because it is, in effect, telling stock analysts to drop dead."

Paul Samuelson, PhD & Nobel Laureate

In my 21 years of advising people who want to conserve and grow their wealth, I have met numerous families and individuals who have had many common experiences. Perhaps their experiences are similar to yours. Here are three real-life stories:

1. I have worked with financial advisers from well-known Wall Street firms who supposedly helped many people find investments that really paid off big. When I talked with them they showed a knowledge of the trends in the markets, provided colorful and historical graphs, and gave strong opinions on what makes a good company, a good mutual fund and so on. But in my case, the timing always seemed wrong. What seemed like a sure bet was anything but. Whenever I complained to my adviser, he would always have an explanation – and then he would try to convince me to listen to him again.

2. I had always heard that investing in individual stocks was too risky. So instead I invested in big name, well-known mutual funds with great track records. I was told that these big funds were the safest way to invest for retirement. In fact, my adviser never really explained all the risks involved. So when the markets declined, it came as a real blow to learn that these "safe" mutual funds caused me to lose a lot of the money I was depending on for retirement.

3. While the stock market was soaring, I decided to take things into my own hands and become a do-it-yourself investor – with the help of the internet. It was fun to open up an account and begin investing from home. While doing my own research, watching CNBC, and subscribing to newsletters and magazines, I managed to invest in two dozen or more stocks. I felt good when I traded online; it was an exciting process, and I felt I was doing the right thing with my time and my money. I even invested in mutual funds that way. Then almost all at once, everything started falling to pieces. Before I knew it, I was in way over my head. I just wanted to break even. I never did. Finally, I decided to cut my losses and get out.

These are painful stories, stories of people losing more than they realized they *could* lose. Financial tragedies like these raise questions about the relationship between investors and the professionals who provide them access to the markets. Questions like:

- What should the relationship between investors and advisers look like?
- How can you tell when there is a problem?
- How can investors determine whether they are being treated fairly?
- How can you know the basic assumptions of those you put in charge of your investment capital?

These four questions head off in a number of directions, and I will address them all from different angles throughout the coming pages. Let's get started by taking a look at the dynamics of the relationship between the investor and the investment professional. Investor Smith needs adviser Jones not only to access the market, but also to advise him on what to buy once he's there. But the sellers in the market give Jones a piece of the action every time he gets Smith to buy something. It's easy to see how adviser Jones might lose track of what's best for Smith, and focus instead on keeping Smith buying. Conflicts of interest build up as sales commissions multiply.

In fact, adviser Jones could go either way. He could give investor Smith objective advice regardless of his reward. Or he could end up seeking personal reward first, and allow his client's interest to fall by the wayside. At this point we have to find out more about adviser Jones. How does he understand his role in the relationship?

This is a key consideration: Does the adviser think his role is *to help Smith beat the market* – or does he think his role is *to allow you to invest in the market in the most efficient way?* The first role is what I will call the Wall Street approach to investing; the second, the "sleep-well-at-night" approach.

It has become commonplace to refer to the bundle of services and salespeople who "plug in" the investor to the markets as "Wall Street." In this book, "Wall Street" refers to the array of financial institutions and professionals who want you to believe that investing amounts to speculating with specialists whose secrets can show you the way to huge winnings.

The individuals who make up this group are Wall Street seducers. Wall Street seducers replace investing over the long haul with short-term speculation; consequently, by necessity, they rely on forecasts and predictions, because their stated goal is always to *outsmart* the market. By contrast, the sleep-well-at-night investor follows a conservative path to the markets, one that is non-speculative, and saves on costs while it scientifically captures the gains of the market within a disciplined plan.

To understand the difference fully, let's reflect for a moment on the opening examples. Horror stories like the ones at the top of the chapter, force people to change their perception of what it means to invest. That is, to avoid these disasters in the future, they need to realize how easy it is to confuse speculating with investing. What is speculating? Greed and excitement drive speculation, and push us to hope that, even though the odds are stacked against us, we can still somehow come out ahead. In fact, Webster's Dictionary defines speculating this way: "...to take to be true on the basis of insufficient evidence."

Wall Street does its best to get you to think of investing as a competition between you and the markets, to believe that you can consistently achieve returns that are above the returns of the market itself. As a result, many investors run from one investment to the next, one adviser to another, believing one fairy tale after another.

Investing: Gambler's game or scientific method

If you take a moment to glance at the headlines of investing magazines or watch the financial news on TV, it becomes clear why so many investors have bad experiences and poor results. Financial news, and the financial advertising that supports it, tries to get people excited, and to encourage them to become active players in the investing game. The upshot is that consumers of financial media walk away with the impression that the potential for gain is great while the risks and costs of such behavior are never fully explained. Robert J. Shiller, a professor of economics at Yale, says the media tells consumers: "that investments can't go bad; that they have the potential to make you rich; that you'll regret it if you don't do it; that it looks expensive but is really not." [1]

Some investors spend their whole lives thinking that they are in a race against the market – that they have to "beat the market." The operative assumption here is that "investing is competing." Of course, many Americans hold competition in high esteem, and for good reason: Healthy competition brings a multitude of benefits.

What is more, the competitive impulse insists on individual freedom, and the belief in the ability of the individual to elevate his or her life by making the right choices. The problem comes when investors apply this way of thinking to the financial markets, where desire to beat the market unleashes the urge to speculate and to gamble. And the costs of gambling are no secret; they include not only the obvious monetary loss, but also the loss of time, a commodity that, though more difficult to measure, is certainly at least as precious.

According to investing legend and investor advocate John Bogle, "the total costs incurred by investors in stock, bond, and money market funds in 2006 came to more than $130 billion." From this statistic, Bogle draws the following salient conclusion:

> Since the record is clear that, over time, fund managers earn the markets' gross returns before costs, that *$130 billion approximates the amount by which fund net returns fall short of market returns.* Yet even as the fund industry

has grown, its appetite for higher management fees remains unsated. In their quest to gather assets, managers organize funds focusing on narrow objectives and market sectors, often capitalizing on the fads of the day at exactly the wrong time. *Result*: *huge revenues to fund managers; staggering losses to fund investors.*[2]

The open question is why so many intelligent, educated individuals pay no attention to the costs they are incurring to enter the market. To say the question is open is not to say that it is a mystery. Wall Street has saturated the investing public with images of gambling and winning.

What is the impact of such images? Let me answer by talking about Kyle. Perhaps you know someone like Kyle. He is "hooked" on speculating. He checks the stock market regularly, subscribes to financial magazines and newsletters from investment "gurus," and never misses "hot-tip" investment programs such as *Fast Money*.

Kyle analyzes the latest report on why this company went up a tic on the market today, and why that company went down a tic yesterday. He spends a lot of time on the computer – surfing the web to get the latest data on what economic trends are affecting the stock market and why. He is not afraid to trade online, and he may have more than one online account.

Kyle can find information on any investment opportunity or mutual fund in no time. Armed with his research and advanced knowledge of the stock market, this investment junkie trades often – always with one goal: To beat the market. Kyle approaches the market like a high roller in a cheap casino.

It is not the purpose of this book to review all the reasons why Kyle is bound to end up losing in the long term.[3] Statistically, he does not stand a chance. Further, though you may not see much in Kyle with which to identify, many mutual fund managers hold the same assumptions, and many financial advisers exhibit the same behavior.

Wall Street makes every effort to tap into your adrenaline, and to foster the belief that the more you read, the better your financial adviser's "exclusive research," the greater your edge will be in your race against the markets.

As for the hard facts regarding the mutual fund industry's willingness to put profits ahead of performance, it is worth noting that over the past twenty years, the average mutual fund investor has captured far less than 50% of the market's actual gains. John Bogle presents the statistics with characteristic clarity:

> Over the past two decades, the annual return of the average equity fund (10%) has lagged the return of the S&P 500 Index (13%) by 3 percentage points per year, largely because of those pesky fund costs. To make matters worse, largely because of poor timing and poor fund selection, the return actually earned by the average fund investor has lagged the return of the average fund by another 3 percentage points, reducing it to just 7 percent per year – roughly 50% of the market's annual return. Warren Buffett accurately describes the problem: "The principal enemies of the equity investor are expenses and emotions." The fund industry has failed investors on both counts.[4]

The average investor had received less than 50% of the markets actual gains. Once you compound the gains of the last 20 years, and adjust for inflation, the investor winds up with about half of that amount, or less than 16% of actual market gains.[5]

How to avoid the market gamblers and start sleeping well at night

Once you decide to stop letting "the Pros" gamble with your investment capital, where can you find the alternative perspective? You certainly will not see it in the multi-million dollar ads run by the big mutual fund companies and online brokers. Those ads play to our temptation to make the big win, and to ignore the risk involved. To the contrary, the alternative approach sees winning as the *taking risks that make sense.* Here the emphasis is not on outperforming the market, but rather on preserving the *capacity to produce* gains.

In his excellent essay *The Winner's Game,* Harvard professor and investment adviser Charles Ellis tells the story of how his mother handled his inheritance. This is his true story:

> My grandparents left $10,000.00 to each of their grandchildren in 1946. While the post-war economy boomed and the stock market rose strongly over the next 15 years, these funds were kept in a *checking* account. Even with 20/20 hindsight, I believe that was the right "investment" policy – for those involved.
>
> My mother knew what she was doing and why. Her father was a country lawyer in Mississippi who went broke during the Depression – like every other lawyer in the Delta region. So, to stay at Northwestern University, my mother borrowed tuition from Kappa Alpha Theta, her fraternity, and then spent the next 15 years typing students' papers at 10 cents a page and sewing little girls' dresses at $1 per dress to repay those loans.
>
> My mother knew how important it was to have enough for college *in the bank.* She was determined her children would go to college, so she wanted to be sure we had enough of our own money to cover whatever we couldn't get in

scholarships. She knew our inheritances would be enough to cover.

To risk that assurance just to get more than we needed made no sense at all to my mother.[6]

Charles Ellis' mother spent 15 years – all the time the inheritance stayed in the bank – protecting her wealth from risk. For her, winning meant preserving what she had in order to achieve a vital goal. If his mother's behavior seems unreasonable to you, you are probably still held captive by the idea that investing is a competition. If on the other hand you see the simple wisdom of her ways, let me suggest that this book – and the style of investing it introduces – is for you.

Many investors do not realize that the investments they have chosen are actually designed around the idea of competition – of quickly beating the market. The key is to devise a comprehensive investment plan that preserves wealth and the capacity to generate more. The sleep-well-at-night investor does not have faith in any scheme to beat the market, but rather in the strength of the market itself over time. This faith, as the following chart shows, has its roots in verifiable results.

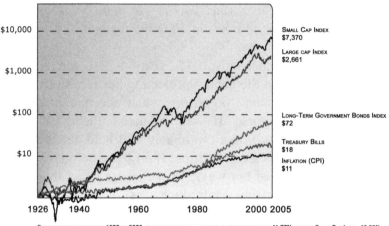

COMPOUND ANNUAL GROWTH RATE OF RETURN FROM 1926 TO 2005

FOR THE EIGHTY YEARS FROM 1926 TO 2005, THE COMPOUND ANNUAL GROWTH RATE OF RETURN WAS 11.77% FOR THE SMALL CAP INDEX, 10.36% FOR THE LARGE CAP INDEX, 5.50% FOR THE LONG-TERM GOVERNMENT BONDS INDEX, 3.70% FOR T-BILLS, AND 3.05% FOR INFLATION (CPI). LARGE CAP INDEX IS THE S&P 500 INDEX®; LONG-TERM GOVERNMENT BONDS INDEX IS 20-YEAR US GOVERNMENT BONDS; T-BILLS ARE ONE-MONTH US TREASURY BILLS; INFLATION IS THE CONSUMER PRICE INDEX. SMALL CAP INDEX PROVIDED BY THE CENTER FOR RESEARCH IN SECURITY PRICES (CRSP), UNIVERSITY OF CHICAGO. THE S&P DATA ARE PROVIDED BY STANDARD & POOR'S INDEX SERVICES GROUP. BONDS, T-BILLS, AND INFLATION PROVIDED BY © STOCKS, BONDS, BILLS AND INFLATION YEARBOOK™, IBBOTSON ASSOCIATES, CHICAGO (ANNUALLY UPDATED WORK OF ROGER G. IBBOTSON AND REX A. SINQUEFIELD)

The steady upward movement of the market over the past 300 years reflects the steady rise in the power of the economy as a whole. This is why you should resist the temptation to get competitive: If you risk it all and lose it, you lose the opportunity to participate in the long-term movement of slow and steady gains.

Financial planning and your values

To invest in the absence of a clear and comprehensive plan is to approach the stock market as an end in itself, a bit like taking your money to a gambling casino, hoping that the right combination of concentration and luck will make your money grow. And it is not news that most gamblers are losers; at the end of the day, the house always wins.

In this way, investing within a competitive framework means ignoring your values, ignoring what is important to you.

On the other hand, investing with values means that you invest as a means to an end – and that end is reaching clear life-goals. These goals are specific to the individual, and are connected to what you decide really matters.

Creating a solid financial plan that avoids the high risks of competitive investing is not as easy as it may sound. The following chapters discuss a number of different kinds of investments, as well as the strengths and weaknesses of *mutual funds*, *index funds*, and *asset specific index funds*. It is vital to emphasize here at the outset, however, that this is only the beginning of the story. There is no way to say, "This investment is right for you," before your values and goals are in clear focus.

In fact, the right investment program for any one person can look very wrong unless that person's values are clearly understood.

Retirees' regrets

A new survey of recent retirees offers sobering insights for investors who envision a carefree lifestyle in retirement. The survey, conducted by Brightwork Partners for Putnam Investments, analyzed people who have retired in the past two to six years. The most important discovery they made is this:

> Retirement doesn't get easier. Some 67 percent of
> retirees said the longer they're retired, the harder
> it gets.[7]

"Many recent retirees have discovered that maintaining their standard of living is much more difficult than they expected," says Merl Baker, principal at Brightwork. "Contrary to some of the common images we see in ads about carefree retirees traveling and volunteering, that's not what's primarily on these people's minds," says Richard Monaghan, head of the Putnam division that deals with investment advisers. "What's on these people's minds is a secure retirement income."

Many investors (led by their brokers) have developed bad habits, habits that cut into their effectiveness in the market. Have you taken an inventory of your investing habits lately? See if you can identify with any of the bad habits in the following list.

9 bad habits of the speculative investor

1. You love the adrenaline rush of making decisions
Daniel Kahneman, winner of the 2002 Nobel Prize in Economics, says "all of us would be better investors if we just made fewer decisions."

2. You believe timing and active trading beats the market
Finance professors Terry Odean and Brad Barber studied 66,400 Wall Street investment accounts and concluded, "the more you trade, the less you earn." Passive investors beat active ones by 50 percent.

3. You rebalance your portfolio more than once a quarter
Various research studies tell us that the added costs and risks of frequent rebalancing actually lower returns.

4. You think that there is a reason for everything the market does
Wharton economist Jeremy Siegel studied 120 big-up and big-down days in the stock market between 1801 and 2001 and found no reasons for 90 of them.

5. You think cheap online trading increases returns
Odean and Barber found just the opposite. And Ameritrade founder Joe Ricketts adds: "Trading often and heavy is not something that makes you a lot of money."

6. You buy when the market is hot and sell when it cools
Morningstar research indicates fund investors are very bad timers, jumping in late and high, and panic selling at the bottom. Rational investors do just the opposite.

7. You're confident that we're in a new bull market
In *Investment Madness*, behavioral finance expert John Nofsinger warns that investors have an optimism bias: "Overconfidence causes people to overestimate knowledge, underestimate risks, and exaggerate their ability to control events."

8. You believe active traders are making big bucks
Unfortunately, even the best winning traders make little for all their efforts, risks and anxieties, averaging about $50,000. Most actually lose money, but deny it.

9. You know you're an 'above-average' investor
Studies actually show that about 75% of investors think they are "above average." Moreover, Boston research group Dalbar's studies tell us that over the past 20 years the average investor's after-tax returns are less than inflation.

If you answered "yes" to 2 or more of these statements, you fall in the category of the competitive investor. Once you stop looking at the stock market as an opponent, you can begin to see it as a vehicle for your journey to the life you imagine for yourself. Once that basic shift in perception happens, certain fundamental requirements come to light. These requirements make up the building blocks of any successful financial plan.

The 5 Building Blocks of a
Sleep-well-at-night Financial Plan

1. Know the resources available for investment.
2. Understand the long-term spending objectives and obligations that will need capital.
3. Recognize and ignore the temptations of the market as it moves up and down.
4. Concentrate on figuring out the long-term investment plan most likely to achieve long-term objectives.
5. Know when to adapt your long-term plan to the *important* changes – changes in your resources or goals.

While the details of these five requirements are best hashed out by an investment professional, his work will mean little until you - the investor - first sit down and answer questions like:
"What is most important to me?"
"What do I really value?"
"What is necessary for me to be happy?"
      Before you can get to any of these questions, you must first be able to determine whether or not a financial planner is a speculator/gambler.

Tax consequences of your adviser's
decisions

      Nothing can take the steam out of your investment plan like taxes that go unnoticed. The losers in the investment game invest just for the sake of investing, and end up failing to plan. Another aspect of this losing mindset is a lack of regard to the tax consequences of financial decisions.
      Astonishingly, many investors – and their advisers – focus so much on finding the "winning investment," that they forget to consider the many ways that the government has invented to confiscate their wealth.

Taxes *cannot* be an afterthought: Each investment decision has to be judged on its merit as a tool for avoiding or reducing tax. Unlike the drama of the stock market's ups and downs, taxes are – well – pretty boring to read and talk about. You will not get many willing conversation partners at the coffee shop if you start talking with passion about tax laws. But this is no obstacle for the investment winners, since they invest to fulfill their dreams, and to achieve their goals, and as a result, they end up sleeping well at night.

Of course, as the glamour of the competitive/gambling approach to investing fades, so does interest in doing it all yourself. But this realization brings a new challenge, i.e., to find a professional Guide who can make the gains of the market available to you over the long haul through diversified and disciplined investment planning. Financial advisers who try to beat the market do not include in their bios that they are attracted to gambling and high-stakes speculation with other people's savings. If life were like that, you wouldn't need the following checklist.

How to determine whether a financial adviser is a gambler

- Do they pick mutual funds based on past performance?
- Do they shop for popular fund managers or trendy funds?
- Do they think outperforming the market is a basic goal of investing?
- Do they often shift clients' investment dollars in and out of the market as it retreats and advances?
- Do they ever charge you a commission when you agree to a particular investment?

If you want to say goodbye to the confusion that equates investing with gambling, that is, if you want to stop speculating and would rather capture the market returns that are there for the taking, you will not want to work with an adviser who answers any of the previous five questions with a "yes."

The adviser or broker who answers yes to *any* of the above questions reveals a larger assumption about what investment advice actually is. The assumption is that financial advice involves the ability to forecast, to predict the future. Would you ever consider trusting your health to a doctor who said you owe him nothing for his insight and guidance because he gets paid from the pharmaceutical companies for the prescriptions he just prescribed for you?

The bad news for these advisers is that no one can predict the future. It is amazing how many advisers out there cannot deal with this simple common-sense reminder. The good news for investors is that you do not need to worry about forecasting the future of the market to be successful. If you do not wish to speculate, why would you look at an adviser who claims to "know" what the market is going to do next?

At the same time, it must be said that there is a deep-seated tendency to fall back into the trap of thinking "this time it's different," i.e., this time, the future *can* be predicted, this time, I *can* outsmart the market, this time – perhaps with the help of an expert – I *can* pick the mutual fund powerhouse that will trounce the stock market by putting a gifted guru in charge.

Wall Street's Legacy

High-cost Failures Designed to Beat the Market

"With all that is known about the poor results of active stock picking, why do so many investors still buy high-cost mutual funds and churn their portfolios? The answer is simple: because they are told to do so, every day, explicitly or implicitly, by the financial media and their advertisers.

Gregory Baer and Gary Gensler, *The Great Mutual Fund Trap*

The idea that mutual funds provide control in an unpredictable environment is reinforced and expanded by the massive marketing efforts that started in the 1980s, and then ballooned throughout the 1990s. In the beginning, stock brokerages channeled the message through advisers who worked on 100% commission. But through the years the message has always promoted the same core untruths, or myths if you like. They boil down to five falsehoods:

Myth #1:   Mutual funds are long-term investment vehicles.

Fact: In 2005, over 200 funds were merged (130 funds merged in 2004). Often, mutual funds are created to capitalize on fly-by-night trends in public preference. When the trend dies, so may the funds.[8]

Myth #2:   Mutual fund money managers are long-term investors.

Fact: The average fund traded 15 to 20% of the stocks in its portfolio in 1950. Over the past twenty years ending in 2006, they turned over their fund portfolios at a stunning average rate of 91% per year – a holding period of barely 13 months for the average stock in their portfolios, reflecting a trading strategy that is far more akin to short-term speculation than long-term investing. For the most part, fund money managers are short-term speculators.[9]

Myth #3:   Mutual fund shareholders are long-term owners.

Fact: The average fund investor stays with a fund for just under three years. Today's rapid rate of redemption – 75% higher than the average rate throughout the 1970s – violates the most fundamental principle of investing success: Buy and hold for the long term.

Myth #4:   Mutual fund costs are declining.
Fact: In 1950, the average stock fund charged roughly three-quarters of a percentage point. By the beginning of the year 2005 that figure had more than doubled.

Myth #5:   Mutual fund returns are meeting the reasonable expectations of investors.

Fact: In the greatest of all bull markets, funds of all sizes seriously under performed the stock market. The inability of 75 to 85% of all fund managers even to match the performance of the market overall is the result of fees, operating costs, short-term investment horizons, and transaction and tax costs.

It was not always this bad. It started out as a healthy relationship: Mutual funds and their shareholders began as two parties making money together. In 1940, the Securities and Exchange Commission outlined a simple rule for keeping that relationship on track. In the Investment Company Act of 1940 one reads:

> The national public interest and the interest of investors are adversely affected ... when investment companies are organized, operated and managed in the interest of investment executives, rather than in the interest of shareholders ... or when investment companies are not subjected to adequate independent scrutiny.[10]

Today, over sixty years later, neither the letter nor the spirit of the law is being observed. This is due in no small measure to the wild popularity of mutual fund investing. With investment dollars pouring into an industry that has grown its assets from $371 billion in 1984 to over $10 trillion in 2006, fund company goals have shifted – from making money for clients to capturing as much of a share as possible from a massive market.

As the billionaire money manager George Soros put it in his address to the Harvard School of Government: "The trouble with mutual funds is that they are rewarded for the amount of money they *attract*, not the amount of money they *make*." When did investors agree to reward fund companies for attracting money rather than making it through sound investment principles?

We will run into a number of unsettling trends and practices as this investigation leads us down many side streets and alleyways of fund management and marketing. We will find, for instance, portfolio manipulation to make funds appear more profitable than they are. We will uncover outdated policies and deceptive marketing techniques that drag down fund performance. And we will find a trade association that fights industry reform as it siphons dollars from funds. In the midst of it all, we will witness the growing costs of these practices to investors.

The pragmatic – and scientific – alternative that I will be discussing has been with us all along, it is just that the din of Wall Street's marketing buzz and hype has drowned out the academics, the Nobel Prize winners, advisers and investors who have come to realize that the gains of the market are superior gains.

Speculating is thrilling. It's exciting to bet on the future. Analyzing the past and then making a conclusion about what will happen in the future provides the mind with exercise, and nothing gets the heart racing like betting money on those conclusions. One of the main themes of this book is that to seek these thrills with your *investment capital* is, literally, to flirt with disaster.

The Myth of Control

When people first hear about alternatives to mutual funds, they are very often confronted with their fear of losing control. One hears remarks like: "I want someone watching my investments, keeping an eye on the market for me. I need to feel secure that my investments will be moved out of dangerous stocks and into safe and growing ones, as the market twists and turns."

Earlier, I introduced five myths about what mutual funds actually are, but the objections in the above paragraph express a widespread belief about the absolute *value* of funds. It is the biggest myth of all.

The belief is this: The constant finessing of a portfolio by a fund money manager gives investors the optimal level of control. This view can aptly be called the "myth of control."

Many investors assume the following: "If I take my savings out of mutual funds, then I would have to manage everything myself. That would be impossible!" People who talk this way have confused investing with actively trading stocks. It is a costly mistake. To begin to loosen the grip that this picture of investing may have on you, consider the thoughts of two giants in investment thinking. First, Warren Buffett, one of America's all time high-performers in the stock market, expresses a view that sharply contrasts with the way of thinking characterized in the previous two paragraphs. Mr. Buffett writes:

> Inactivity strikes us as intelligent behavior. Neither we nor most business managers would dream of feverishly trading highly profitable subsidiaries because a small move in the Federal Reserve's discount rate was predicted or because some Wall Street pundit had reversed his view on the market. Why then, should we behave differently with our minority positions in wonderful businesses?[11]

Next, John Bogle, founder of America's largest index fund for individuals, draws a conclusion in line with Warren Buffett's rejection of active money management. After an exhaustive analysis of the recent trading practices of fund managers, Bogle concludes:

Market timing has thus far been a singular failure, and the rapid turnover of investment portfolios [in mutual funds] has been no more effective. As costly turnover accelerates ... this practice seems destined to become ever more damaging ... the evidence that I have seen shows that the overwhelming majority of mutual funds would earn higher returns each year if they simply held their portfolios static at the beginning of the year, and took no action whatsoever during the ensuing twelve months.[12]

The poor performance of mutual funds

No one denies that the average mutual fund returns 2% less per year than the stock market returns in general. Yet the mutual fund industry spends billions of shareholders' dollars to promote its money managers as experts who can manage investors' dollars with skill. This promotion distracts shareholders from a perfectly simple, and clearly unacceptable, little fact: The vast majority of mutual funds (between 75 and 85% from 1975 to 2005) have under-performed the stock market as a whole·

The following graph shows the percentage of mutual funds that have failed, on a year-by-year basis, to match the returns of the Standard & Poor's index, the most widely followed stock market benchmark. The numbers to the left represent the percentage of all mutual funds, while the bottom numbers indicate the year of performance:

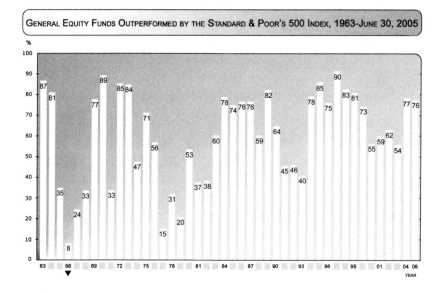

GENERAL EQUITY FUNDS OUTPERFORMED BY THE STANDARD & POOR'S 500 INDEX, 1963-JUNE 30, 2005

With these embarrassing performance figures in front of us, two questions come to the fore. First, with so many mutual funds doing worse than the stock market itself, what are the chances of a particular money manager having one of the winning funds?

Second, what are the chances of an investment adviser picking the winning fund for his clients? Where is the control *here*?

Consider this: In a cover story recapping 2006 and reviewing the prospects for 2007, Barron's reporter Michael Santoli pointed out that US stocks were on track to deliver above-average rates of return but questioned whether investors were enjoying the results since so many fund managers were having a difficult time keeping up with market benchmarks.

"More than 70% of active fund managers were trailing the market as of October 31," he observed. "To have exploited the year's twists and turns fully, one would have had to bet heavily on a commodity boom until May, a sharp slowdown and commodity bust into summer and a recovery led by consumer spending this fall."

In other words, you could have owned a basic, low-cost index fund, spent the year sleeping well at night, participated fully in every "twist and turn" the markets could muster, and outperformed most of the "experts."[13]

Who protects your interests?

By law, all mutual funds must have a board of trustees to oversee operations. In theory, directors of the board are put in place to approve the fund's contract with its money manager, who manages the shareholders' money. In theory, fund boards are responsible for analyzing the fees that a fund charges. In theory, they ensure the fund has adequate procedures to prevent fraud and inappropriate investments. In theory, directors are independent of the funds they oversee.

In *practice*, however, most board directors advocate policies set by the money managers and marketing departments they ought to oversee. Directors at major fund companies often receive over $200 thousand a year to do little more than chair monthly board meetings.

In recent years, high directors' fees have been connected to high management fees. A 1996 Morningstar study arrived at the following conclusion: "The more money the directors get, the more shareholders pay in expenses."[14] In short, the position of the fund director is shot through with potential conflicts of interest. I have yet to discover one piece of mutual fund literature – either in ads or in a prospectus – that says the board of directors has a fiduciary responsibility to mutual fund shareholders. Where is the control *here*?

James O'Schaughnessy was once a well-known mutual fund money manager. He managed four mutual funds with private-client assets totaling more than $700 million. After twenty years in mutual funds, he decided to campaign against them. In an unpublished letter describing his conversion from mutual funds, he cites the following eight problems with the mutual fund industry that he has left behind:

1. Fund fees hurt returns. Many mutual fund investors are hit with a sales commission, an annual management fee and maybe a 12b-1 "marketing" fee.
2. You're stuck with high taxes. Every time a mutual fund manager sells a stock at a profit, you get hit with the tax bill – even if the fund lost money for the year.
3. You have no say. The manager decides which stocks to buy and sell.
4. Fund names can be misleading. The name of a particular fund does not necessarily reveal the types of stocks favored by that fund.
5. Funds change investment strategies. Even when you know what the mutual fund invests in, the fund manager can change direction at any time without seeking your approval.
6. Managers come and go. If your fund manager leaves and you're stuck with an inferior replacement, you'll face taxes if you sell your shares to invest elsewhere.
7. Fund holdings overlap. While you want diversification, you could wind up owning the same stocks in different mutual funds.

8. Funds grow too large. When thousands of other investors buy the same fund, the manager is flooded with cash. The result in most cases is lower performance.

Mr. O'Schaughnessy has taken heat from the mutual fund industry for referring to mutual funds as "relics that haven't changed in seventy years." In the closing paragraph of the letter quoted above, Mr. O'Schaughnessy says that he has been "forced to rethink the logic and sensibility of mutual fund investing." That last remark is an apt paraphrase of the purpose of this book. If the book can force you to rethink the logic and sensibility of mainstream mutual funds, then it has done its job.

Trading Gone Wild

Wall Street Money Managers Can't Stop Rolling the Dice

"More often, support of active management can only be justified by assuming that the laws of arithmetic have been suspended for the convenience of those who choose to pursue careers as active managers."

William F. Sharpe, Nobel Laureate in Economics

The losing proposition of too much trading is this: Increased taxes (from frequent trading) + lower returns (from failing to buy and hold) = unreasonably poor performance.

Too much stock trading in mutual funds not only wounds, but it also pours in the salt afterwards. There are two poorly designed pieces of machinery under the hood of every mutual fund: diversification requirements and the redemption process. Both of these force money managers to sell stocks that they would rather hold, causing funds to choke and sputter. In order to perform well, portfolios need both solid net performance and minimal taxes. By forcing stocks within the fund to be traded, diversification requirements and the redemption process strip mutual funds of both.

The strain of diversification

In and of itself, diversification is a virtue. The idea has been that the success of companies in various industries depends on different economics. For instance, when the pharmaceutical industry has a downturn, the communications industry is not affected. However, legal restrictions force fund money managers to sell the best performing stocks in their portfolios. By law, most stock positions can represent no more than 5% of the entire portfolio; therefore, when a stock starts to soar, the manager must sell it off.

Diversification requirements were put in place over sixty years ago; they have not been updated since. Now consider that the average modern mutual fund holds 130 stocks in its portfolio. Here, the old regulation becomes counterproductive. It flattens the potential for gains from stocks that outperform the market, since the companies hitting the long balls must be sold off right away. The large collection of under-performing stocks dilutes the strong performance of companies with aggressive growth. By adhering to the unreasonably small percentage limit of 5% per company, mutual funds twist the value of diversification into the vice of dilution.

The 5% rule will only affect the best stocks in the portfolio. Since the stocks that have appreciated most are the ones that must be sold, trading to meet diversification requirements means larger capital gains taxes, too. These taxes are spread out indiscriminately to all investors in the fund, whether they have been invested for years or days.

The drain of redemption

When an investor wants to bail out of a mutual fund, he cashes out his shares and redeems them, at their net asset value, for cash. Where does this cash come from? Two places: First, from cash on hand, and second, from the sell off of stocks in the portfolio. Each of these drives down the performance of funds; the second increases the investor's tax bill.

Large amounts of investors' dollars are set aside for investors who want to pull out of the fund. It is unclear how much of your investment has been put to work in the market and how much has been stashed away for future redemption requests. The cost to the investor is that of lost opportunity. Cash that you assumed was at work in the market is actually sleeping on the sidelines. A dollar set aside for redemption requests is a dollar not invested. Inevitably, the cash on hand is never enough, which leads to the second, more painful consequence of redemption policy.

When there is a run of redemptions, managers liquidate stocks in order to obtain the extra capital needed to redeem shares for investors who bail out. Since investors are most inclined to want out in a down market, the money managers have no choice but to sell stocks at low prices. It is only human to occasionally make bad decisions about when to buy or sell things. But what if you had to sell your house at a time when it had depreciated in value, even though it was perfectly reasonable to suppose that, in time, it would appreciate in value? Imagine how agonizing it would be if you had to sell your stocks in a down market, even though you did not wish to do so. That's exactly what happens to a money manager when shareholders start redeeming their shares of a fund. Mutual fund money managers are *powerless* in the face of mounting redemption requests.

In the meantime, the managers have to sit and watch buying opportunities pass them by. Just when they want to hold what they have and to buy other stocks at good prices, the managers are prohibited from purchasing any additional stocks while they sell off what are often massive amounts of their portfolios. In many cases, fund managers will sell rising stocks prematurely, to raise cash in advance, if they think that nervous investors *might* redeem their fund shares.

On one level, the impact of involuntary liquidations is clear. Selling when you would rather buy is a losing proposition. But the beating that the fund's net performance takes by forced selling is compounded by the capital gains tax suffered by everyone who remains in the fund. Of the many shares the manager has to sell, some will have appreciated in value. In each of these cases, every investor who stays will pay capital gains taxes – even if the fund as a whole has lost value. According to Paul Roye, Director of the Division of Investment Management of the SEC, more than 15% of all mutual fund gains are wiped out annually due to capital gains taxes.[15]

Unfortunately, the strain and drain of regulation is only half of the story. To fully unravel the poverty of mutual fund performance, we have to look beyond antiquated policy constraints and the growing tendency to ignore the interests of current investors, and instead focus on how to seduce new ones. We have to investigate the degree to which fund design and management have been reshaped in deference to marketing proposals.

Trading overdose:
Money managers as whirling dervishes

Marketing pressure encourages money managers to trade stocks within the fund's portfolio. In this case, money managers are not legally compelled by regulations, but rather enticed by incentives from their company.

Money managers are awarded for their performance as part of the marketing team. Performance is calculated over periods ranging from two or three quarters to five years, as fund decision makers pit managers against their fund's benchmarks and against one another. The stakes are high.

According to the *New York Times*,[16] the top 10% of money managers take much of the overall pay in the industry. At stand-alone mutual fund companies, managers in the tenth percentile – the low end of the top performers – made an average of $1.7 million each last year, almost four times as much as the median for the group, according to a recent survey by Russell Reynolds Associates, the executive research firm.

At the highest end of the scale are fund managers who double as executives. In addition to the $200 million and five-year contract, Bill Gross, money manager at Pimco Advisers, received $243 million in stock and cash for his stake in Pimco when it was acquired by Allianz of Germany. No matter where a money manager may find himself on the scale, his base salary is only a modest portion of overall compensation, compared with performance bonuses and stock.

Charles Johnson, chief executive of Franklin Resources and co-manager of the Franklin Income Fund, made $1 million last year, while his holdings of Franklin stock rose to $2.1 billion. Aside from high-profile money managers like these, whose compensation has been disclosed to the public, most mutual fund managers have paychecks that are closely guarded secrets. In an industry where the performance of money managers is measured down to the last tenth of a percentage point at the end of the quarter, compensation is a sensitive subject; there are wide disparities in the amount that managers, even at the same firm, can be rewarded. Despite the market's decline, overall compensation for fund money managers continues to rise. Successful marketing of funds means big time bonuses for money managers; it also means high taxes for investors.

At T. Rowe Price, Mr. Kennedy works with the chief investment officer, head of research, and head of trading to assess managers' performance. They review trading and performance records, then ask managers to evaluate themselves. After five to seven weeks of scrutiny, Mr. Kennedy presents his suggestions to a five-member compensation committee. "I never look forward to the process because it's so intense," he said, "We start in early October and the paychecks come out at the end of the year." Here it is important to ask: What is the primary activity being performed for these high salaries and bonuses?

My how times have changed

From 1950 to 1965, the typical mutual fund traded securities an average of 16% a year. The average fund held its average stock for an average of six years. Today, funds trade securities six times more rapidly, while their trading average stands at 100% a year. For fifteen years, the average fund held a stock for 6 years; now the average fund holds a stock for only 12 months.

This frantic turnover amounted to $3.2 billion dollars in stocks being bought and $3.5 billion dollars in stock being sold in 2005, for a total of close to $7 billion in securities transactions. The majority of the trading was between mutual funds. Trading dilutes the returns of the fund shareholders, as the short-term speculators who manage modern mutual funds lose to long-term investors.[17]

Commenting on the costly trading practices of modern fund money managers, Warren Buffett writes: "Fund managers are more kinetic than ever: their behavior makes whirling dervishes appear sedated by comparison. Indeed the term 'institutional investor' is becoming one of those self-contradictions called an oxymoron, comparable to 'jumbo shrimp,' and 'lady mud-wrestler.'"[18] Let's take a look at the gyrations of fund managers under pressure.

Portfolio manipulation

Money managers are tempted to boost their fund's year-end results by buying more of a stock they already hold to drive up its price. Since marketing departments need attractive year-end performance numbers, a fund will give its managers bonuses if they can provide snappy year-end gains. So the manager creates the illusion of a sharp increase in the value of a stock by pouring vast amounts of dollars into a particular holding at the end of a financial period solely for the purpose of fraudulently driving up the value of the fund.[19] This unsavory maneuver is called "portfolio pumping."

Marketing departments want to create the appearance that their funds can do no wrong. Here, the key is to make it appear that the fund was in on the success of profitable companies, while it had nothing to do with the lackluster performance of other companies. This is not a difficult trick. The money manager buys successful stocks at high prices and sells the poor performers at low prices.

Managers routinely buy and sell securities around public disclosure dates to hide their mistakes or to exaggerate their investing acumen. This trick is called "window dressing." Portfolio pumping and window dressing are not only unethical, they are also fraudulent, according to the guidelines of the SEC.

Lori Richards, who heads the SEC's inspections program, has established a task force to investigate the rise of portfolio manipulation in mutual funds. "We are looking for instances of managers window dressing their funds' portfolios to create a misleading impression of how the funds' assets were invested during the period," said Ms. Richards. "We are also focusing very hard on evaluating trading data that would show manipulation – we are looking for signs that stocks may be manipulated at quarters' end simply to pump up performance," she explained. So far, the task force has uncovered thirty to forty mutual funds whose performance rose from 3 to 5% on the last day of the quarter.[20]

Based on his study of mutual fund returns, David Musto, a Wharton finance professor, found that top-performing funds generally posted their best returns on the last trading day of the calendar year and their worst returns on the first trading day of the new year. The hottest stocks generally peaked during the last hour of the last trading day of the year and then dropped within thirty minutes of the opening of the next trading day. The same pattern applied at the end of each quarter.

Musto's findings are consistent with a 1997 study by *Money* magazine that showed that funds often beat the index based on their performance on the last day of the year. The study found that going into the last trading day of the year, 62% of the funds that lagged the S&P 500 index by as much as twenty-five basis points, and 49% of the funds that lagged the market by as much as fifty basis points, managed to beat the market for the year *based solely on their last-day performance*.[21] The improved performance is cosmetic, as any gains achieved are given up the next day. In fact, the trading costs that attend this kind of portfolio manipulation, not to mention the capital gains taxes they generate for investors, grind the overall performance of the fund deeper into the dirt.

Style drift

In the trading that leads up to the two pre-determined dates of performance reporting each year, managers are under pressure to achieve the short-term performance numbers that the marketing department will use to bring in new investors. Often, funds trade in and then out of securities that are entirely unrelated to the fund's name or stated investment style. For instance, that energy fund you decided on could be buying and selling shares of tobacco stocks. Portfolios suffer from style drift as managers wander from one set of investing objectives to another.

Manager truancy is not limited to skipping market sectors. You may choose a small capitalization fund and then, as money rolls into the fund and assets grow, the manager begins buying mid- and large-cap stocks. As if a portfolio with one hundred or more stocks were not unfocused enough, the manager's sacrifice of discipline makes a mockery of the fund's claim to strategic investment.

Not that you will catch a manager red-handed; by the time the biannual disclosure statements arrive, the traces of their manipulative maneuvers will have vanished.

Trading as cosmetic surgery

All of this unnecessary trading transpires so that alluring reports of a fund's past performance can be churned out by the industry's publicity machine. Many studies have shown that even if reports on past performance were objective and fair they give little or no indication of future growth. The required warning label on all fund ads, written by the SEC, states that "past performance is no indication of future growth."

These words – supporting common sense regarding the market's fundamental unpredictability – do not reach to the folly of the numbers proffered by the funds' marketing departments. Those marketing numbers contain biases made possible by the fake – and costly – adjustments to fund portfolios. The real purpose of these reports is not to inform, but to elicit a response that will lead to more assets flowing into the fund.

In his book, *What Wall Street Doesn't Want You To Know*,[22] Larry Swedroe tells a number of stories of apparently high performing mutual funds whose managers manipulate gains in the portfolio in a way that greatly reduces profits. For instance, the Berger 100 Fund, which in 1997 provided a total return of 13.6%, paid out a whopping 33% of its net assets in capital gains distributions. Throughout his book, Swedroe rails against the "self-interested investment moves" of mutual funds. One example he cites is Stagecoach Strategic Growth Fund's decision to pay a distribution of 22% in order to lower the fund's unrealized gains. What makes this a self-interested move? While the distribution may have helped attract new investors, it clearly hurt the existing shareholders by forcing them to pay hefty taxes without warning.

The holdings of a mutual fund are released for two days out of each year. Asset gathering marketers encourage investors to focus on how good-looking a portfolio is when it is put on show. And why not? They have the rest of the year to get ready for the show. It is really a mass marketer's dream. All too often, marketing successes come at the expense of healthy investing habits. Given the year-long darkness surrounding the status of their investment, it is not surprising that investors have flocked to the artificial light of performance reports.

Once an investor class is fixated on performance reports, it is only a matter of time before it becomes common behavior to chase returns.

From the late 80s through the 90s, redemption levels escalated at unprecedented rates. Breaking all records, the year 2000 saw investors redeem a staggering $1,042 trillion from funds. The $1 trillion of redemptions in 2000 represented a 188% increase from the 1997 level of $362 billion.[23]

Think of the increased rate of redemptions as a kind of bad karma. Marketing efforts have been so successful that it is now hard to find fund investors who are willing to sit still. Restless investors are deadly. The only way for managers to keep up with their frequent requests to redeem shares is to sell off more and more shares, lowering the funds' overall performance and triggering increasingly high capital gains taxes.

The tyranny of capital gains

Sooner or later, a fund must distribute all its tax liability from all of its trades to all of the investors. Whether or not capital gains taxes are too high or unfair is not the issue. The issue is the proliferation of taxable events in mutual funds. Investors who buy shares in a mutual fund are also buying shares of accumulating tax liability, even if they were not holding the fund at the time the gains were created. Suppose you invest in a fund just after it has enjoyed a strong run. The fund then distributes big gains. Even though you were not around to enjoy the fund's appreciation, you get stuck with capital gains taxes.

Why have there been so many distributions recently? Two reasons: First, many funds are sitting on substantial unrealized capital gains. According to Morningstar, more than four hundred domestic stock funds carry unrealized gains equal to more than half of the fund's assets. Second, most funds are now turning their portfolios over at an annual rate of over 95%. All of that buying and selling means that built-up gains stand a good chance of being realized and distributed to shareholders. That is why funds can realize and distribute high gains even in a declining market.

Capital gains are taxed even if the full amount of the distribution is reinvested in the fund. A dollar spent on capital gains taxes is a dollar less to invest.

Summing up

It does not hurt a mutual fund company when it increases capital gains taxes by shuffling in and out of stocks throughout the year; the fund company does not pay the extra tax, the shareholder does. It does not hurt a mutual fund company to insist that no stock represent more than 5% of the holdings of a fund; the requirement merely increases the demand for money managers. Finally, it does not hurt a mutual fund company when huge funds provide frequent redemptions to shareholders; the necessary capital can simply be siphoned from portfolios.

Traditionally, conservative trading behavior held the tyranny of capital gains in check. Until the 1980s, trading within funds was coordinated around the principle of buying and holding stocks for the long-term. According to Morningstar, in 1999 the all-fund average annual turnover was 103%. This means that, on average, not a single share of a stock that a fund starts with on January 1st will be there at year's end, and another 3% of the shares that were bought during the year will also have been traded out.

The following chart displays the mystifying rise in fund portfolio turnover.

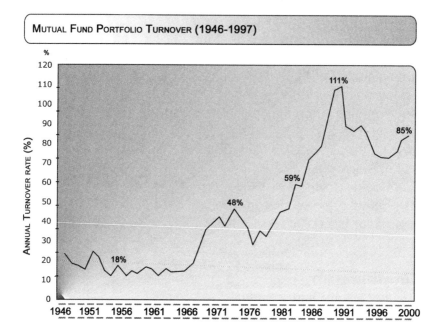

The spike in trading volume reflects the new rapid-fire trading methods adopted by money managers; these new practices focus on short-term speculation on when a stock will go up or down a notch. Erma Bombeck once asked why, whenever there is a traffic jam, the cars in the lane next to yours always move faster. She observed that this holds true even if you change lanes. She resolved to stay put in traffic jams, to refrain from changing from the apparently slow lane to the apparently faster one. Modern mutual fund money managers are like drivers who don't get the joke. They wake up every morning convinced that they will quicken their commute by the frantic switching from lane to lane to lane.

Wall Street's Motto: First Gather Assets

Investment Companies Turned Marketing Machines

"Wall Street's favorite scam is pretending that luck is skill."

Dr. Ron Ross, *The Unbeatable Market*

Much of Mutual fund companies' profitability relies on the hidden business of asset gathering.

The camera pans a buzzing trading floor. Traders on phones. Others quickly moving from their desks and walking with papers. A gentleman in his sixties, in a dark blue woolen three-piece suit, watch chain draped from his vest pocket, steps in for a close-up. Peering down into the camera he says, in the Queen's English, "We make money the old-fashioned way: We earn it." This commercial seemed to run on every channel throughout the 1980s. That old Englishman's assertion provides a guiding light for this chapter: Do mutual fund companies make money the old fashioned way? Do they earn it?

Marketing professionals are changing the way fund companies do business. There are dozens of marketing consultancies jockeying for favor with the major fund companies. Their services are generally the same. The Financial Research Corporation (FRC), to pick one among many, lists the following services on its website: Marketing Plan Development, Mergers & Acquisitions and Due Diligence. These turns of phrase may make the services appear reasonable; nevertheless, their impact on fund companies has been devastating.

The FRC promotes itself to the "decision-makers in fund companies." One of their press releases announced a new study that they would like the fund leaders to buy. The following is a duplication of that press release – material not intended for the eyes of individual investors:

NEWS RELEASE

Is Your Firm Getting the Assets it Deserves?
Standing Out in a Crowded Marketplace:
There is a sharp disconnect between perceived performance and actual performance – particularly among non-shareholders. Famous mutual funds, many of which do significant amounts of advertising, were perceived to have very strong short and long-term performance, whether or not they actually did.

What's more, most investors think of mutual funds in only one dimension: good versus bad. And the primary driver behind whether an investor decides that a fund group is good or bad is perceived performance. The conventional wisdom about actual performance being the primary consideration is wrong. For mutual funds, perception has become reality. Mutual funds that promote strong performance have the best potential for creating favorable perceptions in the minds of investors. ###

The press release does not mince words. The idea that "actual performance" should be a "primary consideration," in mutual fund distribution, "is wrong." The point of the release is to convince the mutual fund managers and directors that actual performance does not matter. Success equals "creating favorable perceptions."

What is the upshot of making the marketing of good perceptions the principle function of a fund company? Placing a company's emphasis on creating favorable impressions, in order to gather assets, leads fund companies to make moves that would never be made by a company whose primary objective is investing. What kind of moves are fund companies making?

The new emphasis on marketing perceived performance is connected to five industry trends that leave investors at a disadvantage. They are:

1. Hyping the track records of the tiniest funds, even though evidence shows their returns will shrink as the funds grow.
2. Creating new funds because they will sell, rather than because they are good investments.
3. Paying money managers on the basis not just of *actual* performance but also the assets and cash flow that come as the result of good *perceptions* and brand recognition.
4. Siphoning dollars from portfolios to provide capital for massive marketing campaigns to attract new investors.
5. Giving negligible warning to shareholders regarding the inherent risks of investing.

Make no mistake: Wall Street marketers *encourage* mutual fund companies to manipulate consumers through intentionally deceptive marketing campaigns.

In June 2006, some big name, actively managed mutual funds applied the FRC's advice with unreserved cynicism when they exploited investors' fears and re-introduced sales loads. That's right. They *RE*-introduced them, having jettisoned them some time ago. Why? As the following clip explains, these establishments of high finance found out that investors perceive that they are "buying" additional expertise when they pay higher commissions. As perceptions go, this one is particularly dim-witted: It could only be entertained by someone who has virtually no understanding of what sales loads are and how mutual funds work. Here is an excerpt from the article:

> June 2, 2007 – Loads come in three varieties: front-end, where investors pay, typically, 5% at the time they purchase the fund; back-end loads, which can decrease with time, depending on how long investors cling to funds; and level-loaded funds, which levy a consistent annual fee, typically 1%. Still, since the bear market of 2000 to 2002, investors have increasingly turned to loaded funds, and industry powerhouses such as Fidelity Investments and Janus have added loaded funds.
>
> The reason companies have begun introducing these less-attractive options is that since the millennial downturn, investors have been more willing to pay for advice and reassurance.
>
> No-load funds are not hard to find, yet investors continue to pay up-front commissions to brokers and financial advisers for advice. But Jim Peterson, head of mutual fund research for Charles Schwab, argues that front-loaded funds are just a way for interested parties to make a buck.
>
> "There's no investment value whatsoever to paying a load," Peterson told *MarketWatch*. Nonetheless, Peterson predicts that long-term stock-market returns will start sinking, and when they do,

investors will start paying careful attention to every percentage point. Loaded funds were far more common when mutual funds were first introduced. But with time, that trend shifted, and the majority of funds stopped charging fees, according to Tom Roseen, senior researcher at Lipper. [24]

And this from a mutual fund industry that has been, allegedly, "cleaned up" after it was rocked with scandal in the early 2000s. Did you know that mutual fund companies also change the names of their funds to hide their poor performance?

What's in a name?

A recent study found Fidelity's biggest funds hold many of the same stocks, in the same amounts, as the S&P 500. "A remarkable 65% of Fidelity Magellan stock holdings," it reports, "are absolutely identical to the S&P 500. Similarly, 63% of Fidelity Growth & Income stocks and 58% of Fidelity Blue Chip Growth stocks are held in exactly the same amounts as the S&P 500."[25] This new sleight of hand, known as "closet indexing," exposed investors to unknown concentrations of risk, as they unwittingly duplicated their investments.

For example: Having invested in a Vanguard index fund to track the S&P 500, you could then place additional savings into a Fidelity mutual fund, replete with money management fees and the other attendant costs, not knowing that all the fund does is track the S&P 500! The situation makes it virtually impossible for the serious investor to achieve a harmonious overall investment strategy.

Until very recently, Fidelity was one of the worst offenders of the age-old scam of selling the name, rather than what is named. It is still commonplace to change the names of funds as the marketing department sees fit, in order to test the market. Note that the fund is not being tested. In order to test a fund in the market, the shareholders need to know what is in it, how it performs, and how much it costs. A messy affair, that. What is being tested in the case of fund name changes is something with a much smaller margin of error: the mass response evoked by the ring of a name.

Before the new rule took affect, it was not uncommon to see mutual funds change their name to reflect popular investment strategies rather than the mutual fund's main investment goal. This kind of name change, however, is largely eliminated today by stricter SEC regulation (discussed further below). These purely cosmetic changes create problems for investors who are pursuing an investment strategy suitable for their current asset allocation goals.

In her book, *The New Common Sense Guide to Mutual Funds*, Mary Rowland dedicates a section to the dangers of paying attention to what a fund calls itself. "Misleading names," she says, "are the product of the funds' marketing departments. If you wanted to sell a fund, would you call it XYZ High Risk? Probably not. XYZ Conservative Growth has a much better ring, doesn't it? Solid yet on the prowl for growth. But the name is designed to soothe and woo investors rather than give them information about the fund's objective."[26] Ms. Rowland goes on to tell the amazing story of the Fidelity Blue Chip Growth Fund, which, from 1993 to 1996, did not hold one blue chip stock! After 1996, when a new manager took over, the Fidelity fund did begin to hold blue chips again. Within a decade, the name referred to three completely different funds.

On Jan 17, 2001, the Securities and Exchange Commission (SEC) tightened their mutual funds regulations: mutual funds are now required to invest at least 80% of their portfolio in the strategy advertised by their name.

One may wonder why the SEC did not make the requirement 100%, which would allow investors to be certain that their entire investment in the fund follows the investment strategy suggested by the name. Mutual funds must maintain some liquidity to meet redemption requests.

A sure-fire way to an uncomfortable meeting with your investment adviser

Once it becomes clear that a broker or investment adviser refuses to budge from the position that mutual funds give his clients the control they need, it is time to ask the following three questions:

1. What is the last mutual fund you recommended?
2. What is its objective?
3. How do you know that the fund has stuck to its stated objective?

Here is a run down of the typical answers:

To the first question, "XYZ Blue Chip Fund."

To the second question, "To invest in the largest, highest quality stocks in America."

The third answer varies, from, "What do you mean?" to "Do you mean how do I know that it's right for my client?" to "I believe in blue chip stocks!" to "It's a blue chip fund; look, here is the name." You get the picture. It never occurs to these advisers that what is actually held in the portfolio may have nothing to do with the name of the fund.

Mergers & acquisitions

In 2005, 511 funds were shut down or merged out of existence. Though the year 2005 saw the most fund liquidations in the industry's history, as the following chart shows, this was no mere aberration caused by a slowing economy.

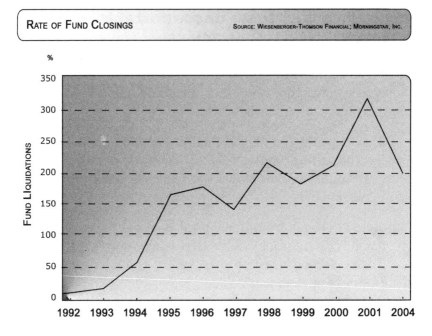

RATE OF FUND CLOSINGS — SOURCE: WIESENBERGER-THOMSON FINANCIAL; MORNINGSTAR, INC.

The chart shows that as the bull market charged through the 1990s, fund liquidations climbed steadily. Funds within the same family acquire one another for the same reasons companies do: to gain assets. The extra benefit to fund companies of these behind-the-scenes takeovers is to give marketers the opportunity to tamper with returns in order to create the perception of good performance in the face of actual bad performance.

The acquiring fund is after assets; it does not care about the fund itself at all. Firms merge funds in their own family all the time. Why bother? Because they want to eliminate the very poor funds before they create too many bad perceptions among potential investors. If your fund is being merged into oblivion, there is nothing you can do about it. Unless you simply divest, and take the penalties of doing so, your money will be moved to the surviving fund. If you are in the surviving fund, the merger means that more assets will affect the fund's investment strategy, and more importantly, its performance.

The impact of fund closings on individual investors

In the section of her *Guide to Mutual Funds* entitled, "Don't ignore a flood of assets," Rowland cites research carried out by John Bogle that shows that an increase in a fund's assets leads to lower performance. "What Bogle found," she writes, "is that across investment styles, in every single instance, as assets increased, performance went down." [27]

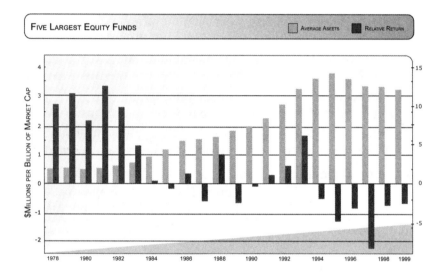

The chart shows five of the largest stock mutual funds whose assets grew from $500 million to $37 billion from 1978 to 1998. Without exception, as assets grew, performance deteriorated. The chart shows their average annual returns, relative to the S&P 500 index, along with their asset size relative to the total stock market.

Fund survivor

In 2001, Liberty Financial merged seventeen of its ninety-five funds out of existence. The announcement came on the heels of the news that Liberty Financial had been experiencing a serious drain on its assets under management. The Liberty case is a good illustration of the industry's manipulation of investors' perceptions. In an effort to stem investor defections from its funds, on October 5, 2000, Liberty began its merger plans. The seventeen funds represented $1.7 billion of investor assets. The assets of the seventeen funds were to be merged into ten existing funds in the Liberty family. The funds that were liquidated had the worst performance. By merging the worst funds out of existence, Liberty magically made the performance statistics of those funds disappear.

The reported returns of the now merged funds will contain only the live returns of the surviving fund. As Larry Swedroe points out in his essay, *Survivorship Bias*, "... the poor returns investors received from the defunct fund did not disappear, they just go unreported as if they never existed."

"Future investors in the Liberty funds," he continues, "are clearly not getting the whole story on the returns earned by investors in the Liberty family of funds."[28] Whether a fund acquires another fund or is acquired, the relationships between the fund, the fund's name, the money managers, the strategy, and its overall philosophy become gooier than they were to begin with.

In 1986, the then existing 586 stock funds returned 13.4%. By 1996, the 1986 performance had magically improved to 14.7%. Twenty-four percent of the funds disappeared. Swedroe summarizes the impact of fund mergers on performance reports with the following remark: "Funds that have poor performance are made to disappear, most often by the fund company merging a poorly performing fund into a better performing one. Unfortunately for investors, only the performance reporting disappears, not the poor returns." Provocatively, Swedroe suggests that the following headline should be an SEC-required disclosure for all advertisements of mutual funds: *Warning: Returns Shown Contain Biases We Are Not Required to Report.*[29]

"The reported returns of many fund families and their funds," he continues, "are often either misrepresentations (intentional or unintentional) of the returns earned by investors, or are at the very least misleading representations. This is because of biases in the data."

Have you ever heard of a tiny upstart company with comparatively tiny capital acquiring a huge and established one? Credit Suisse has merged its flagship foreign fund, Warburg Pincus International Equity into the much smaller and younger, Warburg Pincus Major Foreign Markets. The names sound so alike that, if you say them both aloud, your head can begin to swim. But they are not alike. Not at all. The first one has assets of $403 million, and was established twelve years ago; the second has $32 million and is four years old. Poof! The awful performance of the old and obese fund disappears. Confusing? It's not over yet. Since 2001, the Warburg Pincus Fund has changed its name several more times, and currently its advertised performance is lower.[30]

Minor reforms of a major problem

True, the SEC toughened the rules on names given to certain mutual funds that can be misleading to investors. "It's your right to have names that accurately reflect their holdings,"[31] said former Securities and Exchange Chairman, Arthur Levitt. But the new rule has its limits and loopholes. Regulations slow the corruption, but are ineffectual in arrest.

With competition among the nine thousand mutual funds hotter than ever, playing the name game is becoming evermore popular. Whatever name they may go by, funds are always subject to mergers and acquisitions. In fact, the SEC has noted that a fund's name can still be legally misleading, even if it does not violate the new rule. The SEC has estimated that five thousand funds are misleading under the rule.

Have the new regulations made a difference? There is plenty of evidence to the contrary. Consider, for instance,

Fidelity's recent surge in fund mergers. Niche funds are no longer trendy. Therefore, Fidelity dumps the assets of the once trendy funds into other huge funds. The flash-in-the-pan fund disappears and Fidelity hangs on to the assets it attracted with the flash.

In April of 2007, it was reported that a rash of fidelity's funds "were being merged into funds with slightly lesser results and different investment objectives. That's precisely what Fidelity Investments is doing in its recently announced decisions to merge Fidelity Nordic."[32] The real message here is that marketing has once again trumped serious portfolio design.

Here are three basic questions to ask your adviser in order to get to the bottom of the impact of mergers on your investments:

1. Have any of your funds ever been merged into another fund?
2. Has the objective of one of your funds ever changed as a consequence?
3. Has a merger or liquidation ever caused your fund's performance report to be skewed?

It should give us all pause that the chances are high that most investors in mutual funds do not know the answers to these fundamental and important questions. Why don't investors have the answers? "Okay," you say, "most investors are not interested enough, not knowledgeable enough – after all, that is why one pays an investment adviser." Unfortunately, very few advisers will have any idea of the checkered past of the fund they are recommending. The more disconcerting question then is, why don't most advisers have the answers?

Consider this: if your job is to create "good perceptions," you will eventually consider controlling information. You will try to minimize information that could lead to bad perceptions. In the world of investing, that means limiting disclosure of what stocks your fund actually holds. Keeping investors in the dark has real consequences. Minimizing information lowers investors' chances of charting a sensible investment strategy, and, as the following examples show, it leaves them open to being burned by corrupt insiders.

Switching

Morgan Stanley Dean Witter agreed to pay undisclosed fines and restitution to settle charges that the brokerage firm failed to detect and prevent unnecessary mutual fund "switching" fees.[33] The SEC said the firm's Atlanta office violated antifraud provisions of the federal securities laws after a repeated pattern of taking customers' money out of one mutual fund and putting it into another and charging fees for each transaction.

Each switch lasted an average of only eight months, a few lasted two months, and in some cases money was invested back into the original fund. "The vast majority of these switches were between funds with identical or very similar investment objectives," the SEC document said.

The SEC also said the Atlanta office's procedures, that included obtaining an approval from the manager and client before each switch, were "inadequate." "The commission found that Dean Witter's system regarding mutual fund switching was deficient and could not reasonably be expected to prevent and detect mutual fund switching that violated the antifraud provisions of the federal securities laws."[34] With switching, the denial of full disclosure escalates from mere negligence of investors' interests to enabling criminal behavior.

More fraud?

Legal troubles for Morgan Stanley Dean Witter continued to mount when securities regulators accused the firm of misleading thousands of elderly investors into buying mutual funds that resulted in losses of $65 million.[35] The National

Association of Securities Dealers (NASD), the securities industry's self-regulatory organization, had accused Dean Witter of fraud for the way it sold three mutual funds. Dean Witter sold more than $2 billion of shares in the funds to more than 100,000 investors, many of them beyond retirement age, the association's regulatory arm said.

According to the complaint, Dean Witter told its brokers to promote the funds as safe but higher-yielding alternatives to certificates of deposit without adequately disclosing how much riskier the funds were. Unknown to the investors who were talked into these funds, as much as 40% of the funds' assets were invested in derivatives, whose value sank when interest rates jumped in 1993 and 1994. The drop led managers of the funds to cut dividends, which prompted about 30 thousand investors to redeem their shares at significant losses, the complaint said.

"The problem here is that these are long-term investments and they were marketed to people as CD substitutes," said Barry Goldsmith, Executive Vice President of NASD. "They were marketed as safe, pure alternatives to CDs, suitable for anybody."

In its complaint, the NASD said that Dean Witter sold the funds to "an extremely large number of elderly, conservative investors." About $380 million, or almost 20% of the money invested in the funds, came from people seventy or older. According to the complaints, an additional $154 million came from investors in their eighties, and more than $22 million belonged to people in their nineties.

The complaint named John Kemp, the President of a Dean Witter division of distribution of proprietary mutual funds, and Lawrence Solari, who was Dean Witter's regional director for the Northeast. The complaint's description of their misconduct shows that these two marketers were good students of the consultants of perceptions. The NASD contended that Mr. Kemp oversaw sales presentations to brokers that, "... provided an unbalanced picture of the funds, omitted disclosure of any of the risks and misinformed Dean Witter's brokers about the nature of the investment."

NASD regulators said the main purpose of their complaint is to take issue with Dean Witter's marketing and sales methods, and its strategy of converting holders of insured bank deposits to owners of volatile funds. In fact, while Dean Witter was still selling the funds, the NASD issued several warnings to its members about "sales of CD substitutes and the volatility of these kinds of products," Mr. Goldsmith said.

He added that the penalties could include fines, restitution to the victims, and suspensions or bars for the individuals involved. Along with the $65 million the investors lost, the complaint said Dean Witter took in $119 million in fees and other revenue for underwriting the funds and $7 million annually for managing them. Mr. Goldsmith has said that, after nearly two years, the case is still tied up in litigation, and that until it is resolved, no other facts can be disclosed.

Now, here someone may say, "These corrupt practices are exceptions to the rule. You are making it look like fund money managers and executives are a band of crooks." These last examples are not meant to suggest a widespread lawlessness in the industry; they were assembled to show the consequences of the accumulation of layers of secrecy. Secrecy, not lawlessness, is the prevalent difficulty. Close regulatory scrutiny of the SEC and the NASD makes the spread of criminal activity beyond isolated cases rather difficult. Nevertheless, instances like these show the degree to which a closed system can spin out of control.

There are fund companies that buck these trends and there are vigilant and ethical money managers. The point is not that money managers are hell bent on fleecing individual investors. It is rather that they are all too aware that they must be swift to survive. They balance themselves precariously on the tip of the industry's hierarchy. Just beneath them is the fund's prodding marketing team, which repays the nimble managers by sealing off their behavior from the public. Combined with outsource companies like the FRC, marketing departments have become the driving force behind the modern focus of *attracting* money at the expense of *earning* it through sound investment practices.

In the context of this extreme pressure – from the financial media and the marketing whizzes who work with them – sound financial advice will consist more in guiding the investor around these enticements to gamble.

Doomed From The Start

How the Costs of Mutual Funds Cancel Out Their Gains

There are, in effect, five separate bills that mutual funds charge.

The best way to understand the impact of the mutual fund industry's waste and inefficiency on individual investors is to quantify its cost. There is not one cost; there are five. The five costs of mutual fund investing are:

1. Tax Costs – excessive capital gains from active trading.
2. Transaction Costs – the costs of trades themselves.
3. Opportunity Costs – dollars taken out of portfolios for a fund's safekeeping.
4. Sales Charges – both seen and unseen.
5. Expense Ratio ("management fees") – no end to increases in sight.

The first three costs in the above list have always been hidden. The fourth cost may or may not be transparent to the investor. The last cost, though always disclosed, is rarely fully justified.

Expense ratios average 1.6% per year, sales charges 0.5%, turnover-generated portfolio transactions costs 0.7%, and opportunity costs – when funds hold cash rather than remain fully invested in stocks – 0.3%. The average mutual fund investor loses 3.1% of his investment returns to these costs each year.

Of these findings, Bogle writes: "That may not seem like much, but such costs would consume 31% of a 10% market return. Add in the 1.5% capital gains tax bill the average fund investor pays each year, and that figure shoots up to 46%, nearly half of a potential 10% return."[36] Recent research suggests that Bogle's tax figure of 1.5% is conservative. According to Morningstar's calculations, the after-tax returns of equity funds often are 2% to 5% less than their pre-tax returns.

Salt poured into wounds: Paying taxes to lose money

We have seen that mutual funds are required, on an annual basis, to distribute all of their capital gains from sales to their shareholders. Outside of a non-taxable account, there is absolutely no way to avoid them. There is also no way to predict what they will be, since they depend on the fund managers' sale of appreciated shares.

The three attributes of a mutual fund to keep in mind when thinking about what your after-tax experience will be are:

1. A fund that recently has changed managers. New managers may clear the decks of stocks bought by their predecessor, generating unnecessary capital gains.

2. A fund's tax overhang. This is the amount of capital gains embedded in the fund that will inevitably have to be paid.

3. A fund's turnover rate. A fund with a higher turnover rate generally will have a higher tax burden.

More bad habits: Too much trading

In spite of the low performance and high taxes they cause, trades by managers have increased exponentially. In addition, the industry's marketing machine still lures investors into the same undisciplined investment style by giving them reasons to jump in and out of funds. From the 1940s to the mid-1960s, annual portfolio turnover of mutual funds averaged a modest 17%. In 1997, the average turnover of funds stood at 85%, a *five-fold increase*. In 2005, the average turnover rate rose to 95%.

In addition to saddling investors with capital gains taxes, stock turnover in funds triggers transaction costs. We can only estimate how much funds pay in transaction costs. This is because the funds themselves do not even know the amount. Funds do not keep track of what a stock's bid-ask spread is at the time they are buying or selling it. Bogle's figure of 0.7% (cited previously) has not been challenged and is generally accepted. Unfortunately, rather than protesting the new methods that result in lower fund performance, shareholders have been corralled into the same undisciplined behavior.

We know that marketing departments are being coached to sell the perception of fund performance. The most effective way to do this, studies have shown, is to tout a specific fund only after it has had a significant run up. Huge cash flows can pour into a fund from investors who have been trained to chase performance, making the fund very difficult to manage, resulting in poorer performance.

We also know that the performance reported in ad campaigns is the result of cosmetic changes that were never intended to last very long. As the former chairman of the SEC, Arthur Levitt explains, "In far too many instances, mutual fund advertisements are offering quick returns or instant wealth, but in reality have performances that are not sustainable."[37] If we keep in mind that performance in reality has been proven by market research not to matter in asset-gathering operations, then Mr. Levitt's criticism is similarly unimportant to fund marketing departments. What matters to them is the response that their ad campaigns evoke. And as the following chart shows, the campaigns have succeeded.

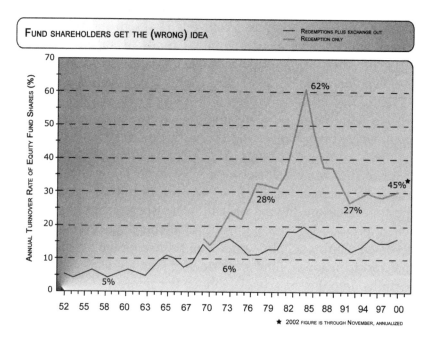

The chart shows that shareholders have become too prone to move investments from one fund to another. Over the past three decades, the holding period for mutual funds has been reduced by 75%. The principle of buying and holding stocks, which was the cornerstone of the industry's practice and advice for the first forty years of its growth, has been killed by the last ten years of bad practice and misleading advertising. In the meantime, fund management fees have been quietly growing.

Inflation built into the system: Expense ratios

Fund fees vary widely. Half of all funds charge shareholders at least 1.4% of their assets each year, according to Lipper, the mutual fund tracker owned by Reuters.[38] That is an increase of almost 10% since 1995, when the median expense ratio of all funds was 1.27%. Many funds, like Alliance Premier Growth, continue to ring up annual expenses of two dollars for every one hundred dollars invested, even as their past gains have rapidly evaporated. And some fund families managed by major institutions, including Alliance Capital, SunAmerica, and American Skandia, have overall expense ratios from 1.8% to 2.13%, according to Lipper. Over the long term, varying fund fees make a tremendous difference.

For example, investors who put $10,000 in the Seligman Communications and Information Fund typically pay fees totaling more than $2,000 for ten years. A $10,000 investment in Warburg Pincus Small Company Growth Fund could result in fees of over $3,000 over a decade, while the same amount invested in Janus Fund would result in about $1,000 in fees over ten years.

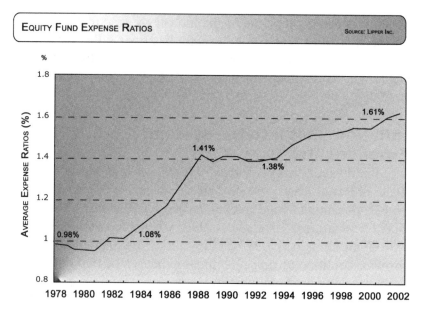

EQUITY FUND EXPENSE RATIOS   Source: Lipper Inc.

Mutual fund fees added up to about $65 billion in 1999. That figure constitutes an impressive jump from the $800 million collected two decades ago. "It's an incredibly lucrative business," said Mercer Bullard, a former assistant chief counsel in the SEC division that handles mutual fund issues.[39] In January of 1999, Bullard decided to leave the SEC to start a watchdog group to fight the new policies of the mutual fund industry that he considers harmful to shareholders. Bullard has found that the profit margins of funds can run *as high as 60%.* Other analysts have put the profits even higher. In all mutual funds, a growth of capital means a growth of fees, since most fund fees are charged as a percent of dollars under management. Fund fees never sleep.

It would be one thing if the most expensive funds gave the best returns. But it appears that the higher the expenses, the lower the returns. By the end of 2000, Alliance Premier Growth had grown to more than $17 billion in assets. Premiere Growth continues to absorb 2% of assets under management. Last year the fund charged its shareholders $375 million in fees. When questioned about the high costs of their fund, Alliance Capital executives insisted the costs were justified by the company's research-intensive management style, which they said produces superior returns. It would appear that "superior" is a relative term in the mutual fund industry.

You say you don't like loads?

The several different expenses associated with funds affect investment returns in different ways, and investors may not understand how those costs will affect them. First there is the sales fee, or "load." Loads may be payable at the time of the investment, or when the investor exits from the fund. Loads can confuse the investor because they are traditionally not included in published calculations of fund returns.

Many funds, of course, have no load. But these funds charge a second type of fee that goes toward the fund's operation, including payments made to the fund manager and administrative expenses. When (or if) investors think about fund fees, this is probably what they're thinking about. These fees are included in the "expense ratio" of the fund. No-load funds may charge higher management fees than their load counterparts, but they also may not.

A recent 170-page study of 8,545 funds, determined that "mutual fund investors this year will overpay Wall Street $36 billion to manage stocks, bonds, and real estate totaling $3.7 trillion."[40]   That is nearly 1% per year of assets *wasted* in unnecessary fees. "This study," wrote the authors, "sought to examine whether individual mutual fund investors are paying competitive fees for money management services. It concluded that investors are not – due to high management fees."

The competition between the thousands of funds is now hotter than ever. As the following chart makes plain, historically, reducing fees has not been a favored approach.

MANAGEMENT FEE RATES OVER TIME (1920-1996, BASE 100)

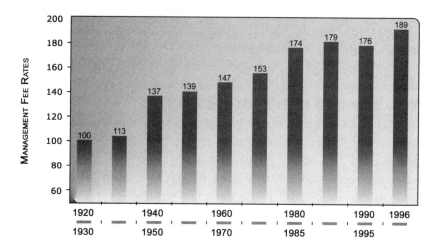

The ultimate arrogance: The 12b-1 fee

In his statement to the U.S. House of Representatives Committee on Commerce, David Gardner, a critic of mutual funds, gave a shining example of what investors face. Of the 12b-1 fee, he said:

> Funds may levy sneaky 12b-1 fees to pay for advertising, marketing, and distribution. This fee, which ranges from .25% to 1.00%, was actually supposed to help investors, under the theory that if fund companies could attract more investors and money, then shareholders would have to pay lower per-share operating costs and a lower expense ratio. That argument was particularly interesting to Smart Money, which noted ... that the Putnam New Opportunities Fund was charging a .25% 12b-1 marketing fee for a fund that had been closed to new investors for over a year. In other words, the investors were paying Putnam $20 million per year to sell their fund to nobody. [41]

For the first time, the fees that the fund companies charged were to become vague and in need of painstaking examination. The fund companies told the SEC that the 12b-1 fee would allow smaller funds to gain recognition and grow their assets. In time, so the argument went, the increased competition among funds would lead to a lowering of fees and, eventually, the dropping of the 12b-1 fee. The numbers make it clear that the lowering of fees never occurred (see figure below). According to Lipper Research Services, there are currently 9,600 stock and bond funds that continue to charge the undisclosed marketing fee.

THE RISE OF THE 12B-1 FEES

	1980	1986	1990	1996	2002
YEAR END FUND ASSETS (BILLIONS)	$135	$716	$1,067	$3,539	$6,391
ANNUAL 12B-1 FEES (BILLIONS)	$0	$0.37	$1.2	$4.4	$7.5

In April of 2007, SEC Chairman Cox said that fund directors and the agency must tackle "head on" sales commissions that are paid to brokers that masquerade as marketing costs. Cox said the 12b-1 fee has nearly been transformed from a distribution subsidy to a "sales load in drag" that compensates brokers. Funds collected $11 billion in 12b-1 fees [in 2006], Cox said.[42]

Mutual Fund Elites & Blindfolded Investors

Investors Pay Their Enemies' Bills

"Risk is not knowing what you're doing."

Warren Buffett

Most investors in mutual funds have no idea what they are invested in, which is the way the industry wants it.

While the media have been increasing our access to information and to the financial markets, how have the mutual fund companies been able to close ranks, and to put more emphasis on marketing ploys than real performance? The shutting-off of information in fund companies has caused quite a stir. There are a number of groups and individuals working to restore meaningful disclosure in the mutual fund industry. How has the industry responded to the new criticism?

In remarks at his final town meeting address in Philadelphia, SEC Chairman Arthur Levitt, Jr. warned of growing unfairness in the relationship between individual investors and mutual funds:

> There are a number of instances that, quite frankly,
>
> do not honor an investor's rights. Instances where
> ... hidden costs hurt an investor's bottom line,
> where spin and hype mask the true performance of
> a mutual fund, and where accounting tricks and
> sleight of hand dress up a fund's financial results.
> [43]

During his tenure, Mr. Levitt devoted most of his written and spoken words to safeguarding shareholder interests, calling for a fully democratized stock market. In his farewell address in Philadelphia he said:

> We have witnessed one of the most powerful and striking developments in the history of the capital markets – the rise of the individual investor ... Remember, these are your markets. You – the individual investor – have risen to become a force America's marketplace cannot ignore. But it's up to you not to give back an inch of the ground you have taken. [44]

The last sentence compares the relationship between the fund companies and shareholders to two armies at war. The analogy fits. Mr. Levitt was an articulate and passionate champion for shareholder rights. He was also the target of constant accusation. Industry spokespersons accused him of seeking the limelight, and of being too outspoken.

The industry's trade association, the Investment Company Institute (ICI), fought him relentlessly on Capitol Hill, dispatching lobbyists to cajole the lawmakers with whom he attempted to reason. Unable to question Mr. Levitt's principles or respond to his detailed criticism, the industry attacked the chairman's personal motivations, and tried to sabotage his negotiations. On the ICI Web site, one reads the following comforting words: "The institute believes that full disclosure in plain English is the touchstone of the mutual fund industry, giving investors the tools they need to make informed investment decisions." The Institute can say what it likes. In reality, it spends shareholders' money to fight against the principle to which it here pledges allegiance.

Pathetic disputes over disclosure

Exasperated by low performance, high costs, and the absence of information about their investments, shareholders have begun to take issue with the mutual fund industry's policies of disclosure. The reformers have tried to engage the industry in a new dialogue of reform. Since the ICI has articulated the mutual fund industry's position on issues for Congress, for regulators, and for the public for over six decades, the reformers thought the institute would be a good place to start. They were dead wrong. The ICI has taken seven swings at the reformers. They are:

1. When shareholders proposed that the industry provide the names and credentials of portfolio managers, the ICI said no. When shareholders took the matter to Congress, the ICI fought it and finally lost when the rule was adopted.

2. When shareholders recommended that the industry provide fee disclosure to individual investors, the ICI said no and lobbied against it.

3. When an open letter proposed more frequent disclosure of portfolio holdings, the ICI said no.

4. When shareholders asked how much of their money goes to the ICI, the ICI refused to disclose the sources of its funding.

5. In response to mounting criticism from shareholders, the ICI wrote: "We have expressed the view that the current requirement to disclose portfolio information is appropriate."

6. In response to rumors that new legislation may be passed to force more useful disclosure policies, the ICI launched a concerted defense against the fund reformers.
7. When Arthur Levitt pushed for clarity in the naming of funds, the ICI fought, and lost again.

Whenever it has faced reform-minded shareholders, the mutual fund industry – via the ICI – has reasserted its entitlement to secrecy with a vigor that would suggest that it is a God-given right. Underlying the assumption of the entitlement to secrecy is yet another assumption: that the interests of the mutual fund industry and of the shareholders always coincide. Underlying that assumption is an ugly lawsuit.

A lawsuit against the ICI asserts that at least half of its dues come out of shareholders' pockets. Shareholder reformers Linda Rohrbaugh and Richard Krantz are suing to recover that money and return it to the funds for investment. Their complaint is that the ICI is run for the benefit of fund companies, not fund shareholders. "The investment advisers and money managers run the ICI for their own benefit, despite the fact that more than 50% of the ICI's funding comes from fees paid by mutual funds that are controlled by these same investment executives." [45]

Ronald Rubin, the plaintiffs' attorney, estimates that $40 million of shareholders' money has gone to support the ICI over the past three years alone. The suit shines a light on an irony worthy of litigation.

Though the shareholders' investment dollars help bankroll the ICI, their voice is nonexistent there. Don Phillips, president and founder of the pre-eminent mutual fund tracker Morningstar, summarizes the association's work this way, "The ICI is by fund companies, for fund companies, and their incentive, their compensation – everything – is to favor fund management." [46]

Mr. Phillips should know. He recently waded into the disclosure controversy by urging that the new profile prospectus, designed to make mutual fund information comprehensible for investors, clarify the role of the investor as shareholder. He suggested that the prospectus begin with the following paragraph:

> When you buy shares in a mutual fund, you become a shareholder in an investment company. As an owner, you have certain rights and protections, chief among them a largely independent board of directors, whose main role is to safeguard your interests. [47]

The president of the ICI rejected the proposal out of hand, suggesting that Mr. Phillips was a crank. "Mr. Phillips is the only person in the entire industry who takes this position," he said. Frustrated by the ICI's refusal to compromise, ten U.S. consumer advocacy groups have petitioned to the SEC to require mutual funds to improve the disclosure of their portfolio's holdings.

Modern mutual fund disclosure:
The great misnomer

Currently, mutual funds are required to show the stocks in their portfolios twice a year; this is all that is left of a once vital disclosure policy. Even these bi-annual disclosures are outdated. Typically, the disclosure lags behind the actual holdings by roughly thirty days. By the time holdings are released to the public, stocks in the portfolio have already been reshuffled. If holdings are disclosed in January and July for instance, the public is seeing a catalogue of stocks that were held in December and June.

In August of 2000, three years before mutual fund scandals rocked the industry, in a five-page petition signed by the Consumer Federation of America, Consumer Action, and others, reformers demanded that the SEC require mutual funds to disclose their holdings more often and have specialized funds increase the percentage of assets in their specialty area. The Financial Planning Association, whose 29,000 members either own or work for firms employing one to four investment advisers, sent the SEC a similar petition. It was effectively ignored.

Fast forward to 2007, and we discover that employees at the 10 biggest fund firms made $1.3 million in political contributions in the 2004 presidential election-year cycle, up almost 240% from $391,938 in contributions by employees from the same firms in the 2000 cycle, according to financial services publication *Investment News*, citing federal records.

The documented attempts of the ICI to squelch investors' reform efforts, through lobbying and confrontation, contradict the image it portrays of itself as a platform for shareholder advocacy.

In a related dispute led by Arthur Levitt, the SEC recently adopted a rule that requires fund companies to disclose after-tax returns for one, five, and ten year periods in fund prospectuses. Mr. Levitt won and the ICI lost. The new rule underscores the growing awareness of mutual fund taxes and how they can affect returns. According to a KPMG study, taxes shave off an estimated 2.5 percentage points from the average mutual fund's annual return, if it is held in a taxable account. That is enough to kill off any out-performance of the market, especially since it will be higher in high-turnover funds.

But the ICI was able to take much of the bite out of the new law by successfully lobbying to have the reporting required on fund prospectuses only, and not in fund *ads*! According to the SEC, mutual funds distributed approximately $488 billion in capital gains in 2004. On the tax-adjustment issue, as well as the petitions, the ICI had no comment.

Fear mongering to avoid clarity

Other industry leaders have said that changes in fund disclosure would make funds vulnerable to competition. "The reason we don't disclose the complete portfolio more frequently is we do not want the street to front-run our portfolio managers," said John Demming, a Vanguard spokesperson. "The primary goal here is to protect the interest of the shareholders," Demming said. In keeping with this line of reasoning, Fidelity Investments has decided to provide even less information. The argument is as simple as it is condescending: Secrecy is safe; information, dangerous.

If the shareholders want more disclosure, and that is not good for them, then less information would be even better for them, the industry's reasoning seems to go. Until very recently Fidelity, which has grown from under $200 billion in 1994 to $700 billion in 2004, disclosed the top ten holdings of its funds on a monthly basis. Never mind that many funds hold hundreds of stocks; only the top ten were disclosed. Look at the fine print at the bottom of any "fund data report" and you will see what percentage of the total portfolio that the top ten holdings actually represent. Some percentages are as low as 11%.

Fidelity spins their desire to keep the wall between the managers and the investors into a fable of customer service. They say, in effect: Some analytical and compassionate minds at Fidelity have realized that this kind of information is hurtful to our valued shareholders. So we made a change. No more monthly updates. If you invest in our funds, please do not ask about them; they no longer exist. It is for your own good.

Fidelity spokesperson Anne Crowly explains that others were trying to capitalize on Fidelity's monthly revelations about each fund's top ten holdings. In any event, says she, company research showed there was little demand among shareholders for information. The coveted revelations of the top ten holdings of each fund are now provided at the more cautious frequency of once a quarter.

The ICI opposes the fund reformers, opposes the shareholders whose dollars they confiscate for their own uses. As of this writing, the association's campaign against reform includes:

- A statement outlining its belief that average investors would be harmed by more frequent disclosure of holdings.
- A legal brief – sent to the SEC – arguing that no fund should be forced to disclose its holdings more than twice a year.
- A study that purports to "prove" that increased disclosure of fund holdings would be bad for shareholders.
- A survey of the institute's philosophy of portfolio disclosure.

The documents rehash old excuses, extending the "information is dangerous; secrecy is safe" proposition into something resembling an argument. The documents all express a fear of widespread "front-running." That is, the fear that disclosure would allow traders to forecast and exploit a fund manager's moves, giving speculators the opportunity to more accurately "free ride" on a fund manager's research and strategies. The worry seems to be that individuals from outside the industry will want to hitch a ride on a dart thrown by a money manager who hasn't beaten a dart thrown by a drunk at a bus depot since 1994. The truth is that real front-running is an insiders' fraudulent game.

That is the way the SEC understands it. They watch out for front-running among money managers, and they prosecute when they find it. When the industry complains about the possibility of others front-running their money managers, they are speaking hypothetically. Essentially, these spokespersons are saying to the SEC, "We want to keep up the wall between insiders and outsiders.

If you tear down that wall, then everyone will be an insider, and everyone will be a potential front-runner."

In fact, secrecy has to survive if the mutual fund marketing machine is to continue to thrive. Myths need secrecy in order to breathe. This kind of secrecy requires that investors give up key rights. But these rights are not for the taking. As Arthur Levitt concluded in his Philadelphia address, "Individual investors are entitled to fundamental rights of fairness, and like those set forth by our founding fathers, these rights are enduring."

Historical Interlude

The Roots of Investing
for the Common Man

Mutual fund investing has its roots in full disclosure and passive money management.

In 1924, an investment company offered the public something totally different. It would later be called the first mutual fund. The name of the investment vehicle was the same as the company: The Massachusetts Investors Trust (MIT). The trust would be an open book to all of its investors. This was a first.

The MIT issued detailed quarterly reports that included each and every one of its holdings, which were categorized, in different sectors, with simplicity and clarity. It also provided full disclosure of all transactions and costs. Up to that time, investment trusts were highly secretive investment pools,

providing personalized service to the very affluent. No one had ever heard of what the new fund proposed.

The new trust added three innovations to the nineteenth century tradition of pooled investing. The MIT would publish its portfolio, promise prudent investment policies, and be self-liquidating when investors requested cash for their investments.[48]

The first quarterly disclosure of the MIT's holdings, issued on July 15, 1924, is reprinted in the following figure.

Securities Owned
July 15, 1924

MASSACHUSETTS
INVESTORS TRUST

ORGANIZED MARCH 1924

TRUSTEES

CHARLES H. LEAROYD
L. SHERMAN ADAMS
ASHTON L. CARR

Custodian and Transfer Agent
STATE STREET TRUST CO.
BOSTON

Amount paid in July 15, 1924
$ 5 0 . 0 0 0

SECURITIES OWNED BY THE
MASSACHUSETTS
INVESTORS TRUST
AS OF JULY 15, 1924

BANK AND INSURANCE

Shares	Company	Cost
3	Boston Insurance Company	682¼
5	Springfield Fire & Marine Ins. Co. . .	325

INDUSTRIAL AND MISCELLANEOUS

Shares	Company	Cost
10	American Radiator Co.	102⅜
5	American Tobacco Co.	145¼
10	Bates Manufacturing Co.	200
10	Eastman Kodak Co. of N.J.	107⅜
5	Farr Alpaca Co.	172¾
5	General Electric Co.	232¼
50	General Motors Co.	13¼
10	Island Creek Coal Co.	102½
10	Lowell Bleachery Co.	120
10	Nash Motors Co.	109⅜
5	National Lead Co.	145⅜
10	Naumkeag Steam Cotton Co.	176¼
20	Punta Alegre Sugar Co.	50¾
20	Standard Oil of Indiana	57
20	Standard Oil of New York	40¼
20	Texas Company.	38⅞
5	United Fruit Co.	195¼
10	U.S. Steel Corp.	97
15	West Point Mfg. Co.	135

RAILROAD AND EQUIPMENT

Shares	Company	Cost
5	American Car Foundry Co.	160¼
15	American Locomotive Co.	73½
10	Atlantic Coast Line Railroad Co. . .	120⅝
10	Atchison, Topeka & San. Fe Ry. Co.	104
10	Baldwin Locomotive Co.	112⅜
20	Baltimore & Ohio R.R. Co.	57¼
5	Canadian Pacific Railway	147⅜
10	Illinois Central Railroad Co.	106¾
10	New York Central Railroad Co. . . .	104¼
20	Northern Pacific Railway Co.	56
10	Pullman Co.	125¼
10	Southern Pacific Company	93⅜
20	Southern Railway Company	60¼
10	Union Pacific Railroad Co.	135

PUBLIC UTILITIES

Shares	Company	Cost
5	American Gas & Electric Co.	70½
5	American Power & Light Co.	261
10	American Tel. & Tel. Co.	121¼
10	Brooklyn Edison Co.	111⅜
15	Con. Gas of New York	68¼
10	Edison Electric of Boston	175
15	Mass. Gas Companies.	71½
40	North American Co.	26¾
10	Southern California Edison Co. . . .	101⅜
10	Western Union Telegraph Co.	109⅜

In this holding's disclosure, next to each stock is the number of shares purchased, or "weighting," and the price of the share at the time of purchase. The structural elements of the trust are transparent. Together, they constitute a picture – the first of its kind, held up in full view for every shareholder – of the clear and simple idea of a portfolio. The picture shows the result of the analytical design of a diversified collection of stocks. It is an invitation to be a part of the collective – to join the group that believes that this is a prudent investment.

Here we find full disclosure. Here also is an effective "capture" of the market. Nowhere is the assumption that some wiz-kid will tweak the portfolio order to beat the market. It would be nearly 40 years before such nonsense was even discussed in the halls of the country's investment companies.

The birth of the "fish-bowl" tradition

Before the MIT, most of the financial industry believed that the details of the trusts it oversaw were confidential information, for fund company executives only. With the introduction of the new investment device, which would later be called the mutual fund, each investor would also be a shareholder, to whom the money managers would be accountable. The unique offer was a quantum leap in the evolution of investment vehicles that would provide a hedge against inflation for individuals and families. But first there would be corruption and pain. The MIT was roughly two decades ahead of its time.

Toward the end of the bull market of the 1920s, money managers began borrowing heavily against the securities in their secretive portfolios. When the market crashed, the older-style trusts were ruined. Many of these investment companies were flagrantly dishonest operations, and all of their operations were kept secret. The falling apart of the institution made it do things it was not meant to do. The SEC intervened. They drew up the Investment Company Act of 1940, which has functioned as a constitution for investment trusts and mutual funds to the present day. The constitution's objective was (and is) to protect shareholders from investment companies.

In its new constitution for shareholders, the SEC turned the best principles and policies of the investment industry into legally binding regulations. The SEC returned pooled investing to the straight and narrow by revisiting the inventions of the

MIT. The SEC made the three main innovations of the MIT the three pillars of new regulation. The innovations were published portfolios, self-liquidation, and the promise of prudent trading practice. The SEC referred to them as full disclosure, redemption policy, and diversification requirements. (Note: the one regulation that did the most good, and was thought of most highly – full disclosure – is the same one that is under siege today.)

A *Time* magazine article in 1959 called the disclosure guidelines "the great 'Fish-Bowl' policy." The article reported that:

> Despite howls from the financial world, The Massachusetts Trust opened its books and portfolio of stocks to the public, setting the pattern for the 'Fish-Bowl' policy under which the whole fund industry now operates. Instead of fighting New Deal legislation aimed at regulating investment company practices, it recognized the need for regulation and helped the New Deal frame the laws. So similar were the MIT's bylaws to the Investment Company Act of 1940, which laid the ground rules for the funds, that MIT had to change only a few commas.[49]

As late as 1959, *Time* magazine could report that the "whole industry" continued to operate under the policies of full disclosure. The Fish-Bowl policy was seen as a necessary feature of an investment vehicle whose purpose was to pave a highway to the profitability of investing for elite and non-elite alike, making the savings of working people finally mean something.

In this same *Time* article, money manager Dwight Robinson was asked about his trading practices. "The Massachusetts Trust never puts more than 5% of its assets into one company, or more than 25% into one industry."[50] Here we find a sample of the second MIT investment principle that the

SEC wrote into its new constitution, with the words "diversification requirements." With the corrupt reaction of fund managers to the Great Depression fresh in their minds, the regulators quickly took to the idea of mandatory diversification of portfolios. But it is important to notice that the managers of the MIT connected diversification to a more perennial investment principle, i.e., buying and holding. Mr. Robinson told *Time* magazine that, "Since the Trust buys for the long pull, it is not bothered by short-term fluctuations. When the market turns down, we just try to ride it out."[51]

With what we have seen of the trading practices of modern mutual funds, it is hard to believe that this remark came from a fund money manager. But then, things were very different in 1959. Not only was full disclosure an absolute, but so too were crystal clear fees, and sensitivity to the taxes caused by trading within a portfolio.

In fact, there were other trusts during the same time period that felt the MIT was not taking the principle of buying and holding seriously enough. In 1938, Founders Mutual Fund introduced itself as a more disciplined alternative to The Massachusetts Investor's Trust.[52] To improve upon the MIT, Founders would be a "fixed trust," and *freeze* its holdings indefinitely. They picked an equal-weighted portfolio of thirty-six blue chip stocks and held them until 1983! At the end of that forty-five-year period, Founders owned the same thirty-six stocks it had owned at the outset.

The record shows that MIT and Founders both earned an average annual pretax return of 10.3%. But Founders distributed negligible capital gains, while MIT's trading prompted very large ones. In other words, Founders was the clear out performer after taxes. Another fund to follow the "frozen holdings" philosophy was Lexington Corporate Leaders Fund, formed in 1935. Over the past twenty-two years, the fund has virtually matched the S&P 500 index, placing it in the top 1% of mutual fund performance. Of these findings, John Bogle has remarked: "A fund selecting a fixed initial list of large stocks –

and holding it, come what may – can give a fully competitive account of itself on an after-expense, after tax basis. By so doing it can generate a substantial margin of after-tax advantage relative to other funds."[53]

The death of the "fish-bowl"

Today, the mainstream fund industry has drifted light years away from its founding principles. In the year 2005 for instance, the average mutual fund portfolio turnover rate was roughly 95%; when Mr. Robinson was interviewed in 1959, it was 20%. Secrecy has regained the status of an industry entitlement. Now everything is hidden: trades, holdings, operations, and fees. Meanwhile, fees increase while expensive, hyperactive trading within portfolios continues unabated. The innovations of disclosure and the convention of buying and holding stocks in a portfolio survived intact for four decades; nevertheless, today, the industry denies the most critical aspects of its commendable "fish-bowl" tradition.

With its emphasis on diversification and discipline, buying and holding for the long term, rejection of gambling and the hype that surrounds it, the new index investing restores the core principles of the mutual fund founders, and gives us reason to hope for future generations of American investors.

Sleeping Well At Night

Build Wealth by Making the Capital Markets Your Ally

"The investor's chief problem – and even his worst enemy – is likely to be himself."

Benjamin Graham
Author, *The Intelligent Investor*

The First Smart Investment Alternative: Index Funds

The point that the index fund makes is this: even if money managers worked for free, they still would be too expensive.

The pioneers of the indexing concept were William Fouse and John McQueen of Wells Fargo Bank. From 1961 to 1971, they had worked from academic models to develop the principles and techniques that led to index investing. The idea,

so simple that it sparked controversy, was to provide a broad-
market index fund that would match as closely as possible
the return of the overall stock market. The concept would be
tweaked for several years, until, in 1976, they offered an index
fund with a market-weighted strategy using the S&P 500
Composite Index.

It was into the community of these ideas that John Bogle
introduced the index fund for the individual investor. The mutual
fund industry was not amused. In the 1970s, the industry was
doing everything it could to lure investors back after the dismal
end of the 1960s. This meant developing a sea of new mutual
funds, and introducing a school of new money managers.
Attracting and keeping investors in funds would require a general
confidence in the acumen of the new money managers.

A story about how funds would actually perform better
without the slick money managers was the last thing industry
leaders wanted to hear. But that was John Bogle's story.

Mary Rowland shared the following anecdote from a
conversation with Mr. Bogle: "John Bogle told me years ago that
he 'used up the shoe leather in three pairs of shoes' trying to get
someone to agree to help him raise money for his first index
fund, which was considered 'un-American' on Wall Street in the
1970s."[54] Bogle was determined to provide individual investors
with a pooled investment that represented all of the stocks in the
S&P 500 (the stocks of 500 leading companies in leading
industries). The argument for index investing is an argument
against actively managed money. This is an argument that Bogle
had been following for years.

Perhaps the most amazing aspect of Bogle's amazing
investment vehicle is that it is not amazing at all. Bogle's
Vanguard 500 Index Fund is no more than a broadly diversified
portfolio, run at rock-bottom costs, without the supposed benefit
of a star money manager. The Dow, the S&P 500, the Nasdaq
100, and the Wilshire 5000 are all indexes. Each is a group of
stocks chosen to represent portions of the stock market. The
index fund simply buys and holds the securities in a particular

index, in proportion to their weight in the index. Given that the Standard and Poor's 500 Index has outpaced 96% of all actively managed mutual funds, a fund that mirrors the S&P looks like a far better bet than one that tries to beat it.

In 1974, John Bogle founded Vanguard, the company that would distribute the country's first index fund, the Vanguard 500. On August 31, 1976, he established the first index fund for individual investors. The ability to index, with its inherent benefits, had always been reserved for the big institutions. Yet the facts were never clearer. With the majority of mutual funds failing to consistently keep up with the market's overall performance, an index fund for individuals that would keep pace, was overdue.

Index investing: The mirror of the markets

John Bogle once likened the stock market to a garden, marked by seasons of growth and decline, with its roots remaining strong. "Despite the changing seasons," he said, "our economy has persisted in an upward course, rebounding from the blackest calamities." If the market is a garden, then indexes are the ongoing records of the activity in one section of the garden or another. An index investment vehicle is like a mirror, held up to a particular record of the garden's growth. An investor in such a vehicle holds up the mirror to a part of the garden and says, "That's it, that is what I have invested in." The quintessential buy-and-hold investment, indexing illustrates an abiding faith in the long-term health of the markets.

The consensus: Active money management is a management a fool's errand

Bogle recalls the time in recent history when the idea of index investing began to spread from academia to the first professional believers. Here are two quotes that illustrate the enlightenment that Bogle ushered in:

The investment management business is built upon a simple and basic belief: Professional managers can beat the market. That premise appears to be false.

Charles Ellis, Managing Partner of Greenwich Associates
in "The Loser's Game," Financial Analyst's Journal *(July/August 1975).*

While funds cannot consistently outperform the market, they can consistently under-perform it by generating excessive research (i.e., management fees) and trading costs ... it is clear that prospective buyers of mutual funds should look over the costs before making decisions ... mutual funds actually do worse than the market.

A.F. Ehbar, Associate Editor of Fortune magazine,
"Some Funds Make Sense," Fortune *Magazine*
(July 1975).

The evidence continues to mount. The *Journal of Private Portfolio Management* contained a study that looked at the odds of active managers outperforming the S&P 500.[55] The study looked at all 307 large-cap funds with at least a ten-year history. This kind of review creates "survivorship bias": Funds that perform poorly typically either close because of redemptions by investors or get merged out of existence. Either way, the more embarrassing performance data disappears. The study was only examining the *better* performing funds over the last decade. The other funds have vanished from the face of the earth.

It is astonishing that *in spite* of the unfair handicap against it in the study, the S&P 500 still consistently pummels actively managed funds. Over a twenty-year period the S&P outperformed over 93% of all *surviving* funds. For a fifteen-year period it outperformed actively over 99% of all surviving funds. For ten, seven, five, and three-year periods the passive strategy outperformed at least 95% of all surviving active funds. Keep in mind also that this is all on a pre-tax basis.

Taxes: The sleeping giant

In his discussion on taxes, Bogle cites a comparison, by James Garland, of the after-tax returns of an investor in a typical mutual fund and a tax-sensitive index fund. Mr. Garland observed, "Taxable investing is a loser's game. Those who lose the least – to taxes an – stand to win the most when the game's all over."[56] After expenses and taxes, the average mutual fund compounded at 8.0%, and the tax-managed fund compounded at 10.2%.

When Vanguard introduced its first index fund to individual investors in 1976, it hoped to launch with $150 million; by year's end, the first index fund only managed to garnish a disappointing $11.4 million in initial underwriting. In 2000, John Bogle's Vanguard 500 was one of the nation's largest funds, with more than $100 billion in assets. About 12% of the money invested in diversified U.S. stock funds sat in index portfolios, according to fund-tracker Lipper Inc., and among pension funds, indexing accounts for perhaps 25% or 30% of assets, according to estimates.

September 2005 marked the thirtieth anniversary of the creation of the first index mutual fund. The evidence on the triumph of indexing is overwhelming. In the mutual fund industry, total assets of equity index funds, barely $1 billion in 1990, now total over $550 billion, one-sixth of all equity fund assets.

While that first index fund of 1975 wasn't copied until 1984, nearly a decade later, there are now 430 equity index funds, and even 30 bond index funds. In the pension world, where the idea of indexing took hold several years earlier than in the fund field, the indexed assets of corporate, state and local retirement plans, $900 billion in 1990, now total $3 1/2 trillion.

Combined indexed assets – linked to U.S. and international stock and bond indexes – of mutual funds and retirement plans now exceed $4 trillion. Indeed, three of America's ten largest money managers (State Street Global Advisers, Barclays Global Investors, and Vanguard, all overseeing from $700 billion to $1 trillion in assets) have reached this pinnacle largely on the basis of their emphasis on index strategies.[57]

Not surprisingly, the mutual fund industry began churning out a wide variety of index funds as soon as they were convinced of their popularity. Which brings us to a broader difference between index funds and mutual funds.

Index funds are what they are

Index funds are what they are and they are not another thing. An odd way to describe an investment vehicle? Perhaps. But a moment's reflection on the changes in mutual funds reveals that mutual funds are not what they say they are and are always ready to become something else.

For years the big brokerage houses avoided index funds like the plague, fearful that they would hurt regular brokerage business. Most but not all of them have jumped on the index fund bandwagon. Back in the late 1970s for instance, Fidelity Investments chief Edward Johnson III expressed disdain for the indexing idea. "I can't believe," he said, "that the great masses of investors are going to be satisfied with just receiving average returns." A decade later, in 1988, Fidelity launched its first index fund for retirement plans. Three years after that, it launched its first full-fledged index fund to individual investors.

Yet even today Fidelity Senior Vice President touts the old-party line when asked about the implications of indexing's success for the very idea of active fund management. "We as a company," says Sarah Libbey, "definitely stand behind active management as being what over the long term will produce the best results." Of course, if her belief were valid, or if it were even taken seriously within her own company, Fidelity would not be invested as heavily as it is in index funds. Which is it? Are index funds a good idea or a bad idea? Fidelity is talking out of two sides of its mouth.

The case against the mutual fund industry is not about index funds. It has to do with money managers, disclosure policies, marketing departments, fee structures, the pain of unnecessary taxes, and, of course, heightened expectations accompanied by disappointing performance. The mutual fund industry's co-opting of the index fund market can make it easy to forget that index funds were introduced as an *answer to problems endemic to mutual funds*. Do not be confused. Mr. Bogle looked to the interests of the individual investor; the fund companies looked to their own.

Index funds *are* a viable alternative to mutual funds; their viability resides in how they *differ* from mutual funds, not in any cosmetic similarity. It is wrong to focus on the similarities of these two investment vehicles when the differences are what matter to the shareholders.

John Bogle's index fund had been germinating in his mind since 1949, when, as a senior at Princeton, he happened upon a magazine article covering the obscure industry of mutual funds. Perhaps the small industry struck the young Bogle as enigmatic; perhaps it was its novelty. Whatever caught his attention certainly stuck there. Bogle devoted his senior thesis to describing the role of mutual funds in America, and has spent the last fifty years detecting and describing variations of its basic conclusion.

Summing up: The lessons of index funds

Half a century after he wrote his thesis at Princeton, Bogle returned to his central conclusion, while criticizing the waning integrity of the mutual fund industry.

As I write these words, I am struck by their
similarity to the bedrock principle of the mutual
fund industry ... cited almost fifty years ago in my
senior thesis: 'The principle function of investment
companies is the supervision of their portfolios.
Everything else is incidental to the performance of
this function.' It is high time we renewed this
mission.[58]

Here is the insight that provided the vivid core of Bogle's
vision of the index fund; it is the belief that had him wearing out
his shoes to find backers in the early 1970s.

The index fund is the precursor to mutual fund alternatives
precisely because it lifts individual portfolio investing out of the
mire of too much trading, undisclosed holdings, and a flat
disregard for taxes. The lesson of index investing provides (at
least) seven essentials. Any investment vehicle should:

1. Facilitate long-term investing.
2. Be supervised by long-term institutional investors.
3. Discourage short-term ownership.
4. Keep costs down by keeping turnover to a minimum.
5. Minimize taxable events with clear tax policies.
6. Identify sectors of the market, seek diversification, and
   stick to its objectives.
7. Provide easy access to information necessary to make the
   above determinations.

We have a responsibility to pursue alternatives that abide by
these lessons. Bogle saw not only the responsibility to move
beyond mutual funds, but also the opportunity to do so
profitably.

The next step in index investing:
Institutional Asset Class Funds

There is a way of investing that blends the common wisdom of index funds with the latest information technology and recent financial science. The wisdom of index funds investing lies in the belief that markets build wealth over time and the understanding of the need to diversify across a broad range of stocks. Well, asset class investing manifests this belief and this understanding in spades, by providing investors with a wider range of strategies to gain greater expected returns – all within the bounds of indexing.

Though they are quite similar to generic index funds, institutional asset class funds have some distinct advantages – features that increase the likelihood of better returns over time. In fact, academic research strongly suggests that the expected returns in a structured portfolio using asset class funds may be as much as 2-3% above the returns available utilizing generic index funds. Of course, there are reasons for these expectations of higher returns.

Let's begin with a clear definition. As generic index funds are built to mirror and mimic a specific index (S&P 500, Wilshire 5000, etc.), these indexes, although doing a good job of representing asset classes such as Large Cap, Small Cap, etc., neglect other, more subtle asset classes, particularly international ones.

Today, asset class fund managers have new tool-sets at their disposal that allow for increased flexibility, so they no longer have to be slaves to the decisions of this or that index. This new control goes straight to the bottom line: the passive fund manager can now keep transaction costs at a minimum, and can weigh the tax consequences of trading before he buys or sells anything.

The asset class investor is not content to simply hold all the stocks in a particular index. For one thing, whether or not an index decides to drop this stock or add that one has to do with the guidelines of the index. Such a decision has nothing to do with what would be best for investors who have "bought into" that index through an index fund. So mirroring the index to a "T" can lead to wasted energy, as the passive fund manager buys and sells stocks merely to make sure that the index fund looks just like the index it tracks.

The second advance that asset class funds make is external, in that they exploit recent global information systems to efficiently expose the individual investor to capital markets across the globe. These two innovations combine with breakthroughs in financial science to allow the individual investor to balance stocks, bonds and targeted asset classes for a comprehensive investment plan. When positioned with care, additional asset classes reduce risks in a portfolio as they increase the chance for increased gains by reaching out into asset classes unavailable to the generic index fund.

At this point, I want to reiterate that these innovations within the indexing model are *not* parts of a new method for beating the market. This is not passive portfolio management that sneaks in active management when no one is looking.

Rather, this is passive investing at its most meticulous and scientific. This is passive investing that alerts itself to *all* of the information the market has to offer. Generic index funds can lack flexibility: Their only objective is to own, sell, and buy whatever the index it is mirroring. In contrast, the objective of asset class is to mirror a certain asset class (Large Cap, Int'l, Small Cap, Micro Cap, etc.), while remaining free of the constraints of tracking precisely a certain index.

In moving ahead to focus on the subtle complexity of asset classes the world over – and how to capture their gains – we also move back, to a clearer, simpler investment style – one that exhibits the same common wisdom of the original index fund. This is a wisdom that says the slow and the steady win the day over the fast and furious.

Remember, the central principle of the first smart alternative to mutual funds is that market returns are superior returns. This principle says, in effect, that you could pile up every scheme and strategy that has been designed to beat the market, from the dawn of corporate investing to today, and it would amount to nothing more than a monument of falsehoods, built up as a tribute to the folly of man, a testament to his proclivity to take his marching orders from fear and greed.

The common wisdom at issue here is akin to the simple truth of Aesop's fable of the tortoise and the hare. This wisdom transcends the moral of the classic children's story of course, and cuts deep into the nature of investing, as it impinges on saving, conserving, planning for the future and persevering. It should come as no surprise then, that the intuitive "sense" that index investing makes has been born out by scientific research.

Behind the scenes: Nobel prizes, advanced information systems and financial science

Asset class investing continues to be developed and advocated by financial economists from Universities across the globe, including Harvard, Yale, Stanford, Dartmouth and the University of Chicago. These academics lead the way in understanding risk and return in today's capital markets.

In order to deliver the gains of the capital markets to individual investors, advisers and academics have established a community of ideas dedicated to investment success. The community includes academic leaders in the field of asset pricing, who find new sources of risk and return in advance of the industry, as well as researchers who engineer strategies and bring client feedback to these financial economists for further testing and enhancements.

In this way, empirical research becomes more relevant to practical investing, and practical investing is backed by solid theory and economic knowledge. This is a continuous process to which the new passive index fund managers commit substantial resources, bringing increasing relevance and new opportunities to the development of science and practice.

The guiding light of this flagship of serious pooled investing is a logical argument based on empirically verifiable propositions. It is known as the "efficient markets hypothesis" (EMH). The efficient market hypothesis states that it is not possible to consistently outperform the market by using any information that the market already knows, except through luck. Information or news in the EMH is defined as anything that may affect prices that is unknowable in the present and thus appears randomly in the future.

The efficient market hypothesis asserts that financial markets are, more or less, "informationally efficient," or that prices on traded assets, e.g., stocks, bonds, or property, already reflect all known information and therefore are unbiased in the sense that they reflect the collective beliefs of all investors about future prospects. Professor Eugene Fama at the University of Chicago Graduate School of Business developed EMH as an academic concept of study through his published Ph.D. thesis in the early 1960s at the same school.

The idea that the price of a security reflects all the knowledge and expectations of investors is based on an understanding of the nature of all markets. In short, a market, any market, is a mechanism of information. In this light, you can see the hubris that is written into the active fund manager's quest to beat the market.

When a manager buys or sells a so-called "mis-priced security," in effect he claims to see something that millions of other investors, (all with access to the same information) do not. As Rex Sinquefield of Dimensional Fund Advisers puts it, "when an active manager buys or sells a security he believes that in this instance the free market or capitalism is not working." Or in other words, for this active manager to be right, the market must fail, (i.e., because he thinks the market is not pricing this security accurately to reflect its true worth and will try to capitalize upon that opportunity with your money).

Other empirical evidence comes from studies showing that the return of market averages exceeds the return of actively managed mutual funds. Thus, to the extent that markets are inefficient, the benefits realized by seizing upon the inefficiencies are *outweighed by the costs involved in finding them, acting upon them, advertising, etc.*

Today, through technological advances, new information is readily available to all investors. Financial markets have become incredible information processing machines and data is almost instantly reflected in securities prices. Now markets are so competitive that it is unlikely any single investor can routinely profit at the expense of all other investors.

Of course in any given period, by chance, an active manager might guess right. But over time, very few active managers have demonstrated an ability to consistently beat the market. Many have "blown up," and lost significant client assets. Again, to quote Sinquefield: "So who still believes markets don't work? Apparently it is only the North Koreans, the Cubans, and the active managers."

The efficient markets hypothesis provides a logical and empirical justification of the common wisdom discussed above. John Bogle accepts the hypothesis, as does the community of academics who have developed the only integrated network for passive asset class funds, *Dimensional Fund Advisors.* (Indeed, one of the members of this community is Dr. Fama himself, the economist who constructed the hypothesis.)

It is worth noting that the difference between the original indexing of *Vanguard* and the more sophisticated asset class investing of *Dimensional* shows itself in the different ways that each passive money management company provides access to their funds. While the individual investor can purchase shares of *Vanguard* index funds directly, *Dimensional* asset class funds are available only through fully qualified investment advisers.

The relative inaccessibility of *Dimensional's* asset class funds reflects the managers' sensitivity to portfolio turnover and its consequences for the shareholders' bottom line. The founders of *Dimensional* believe that individual investors with bad habits can jeopardize the long-term performance of a fund as they pop in and out of funds in their vain attempts to chase performance. A lack of investor discipline can generate extra taxes for remaining shareholders, add transaction costs, and generally dilute fund performance by triggering redemptions. (In fact, Bogle has said the same thing on more than one occasion, even though the company he founded, *Vanguard*, has yet to prohibit individual access to their funds.)

Dimensional's policy also demonstrates its abiding belief in the overriding value of professional guidance. Let's take a closer look at this way of thinking.

The need for guidance: *Investment* performance vs. *investor* performance

Once you grasp what investment advisers cannot do, what they *can* do becomes less mysterious. Advice becomes more a process of consultation, to help the individual gain clarity on his personal goals, and to bring discipline to the process, especially when the inevitable downturns show up, and the gurus and pundits crowd the airwaves with their elaborate stories of the riches to be had by moving your investment capital from here to there.

An investment plan that delivers the performance of the market must take into account the wide gap that exists between the performance of an investment and the performance of the investor. For example, while the market has had a return of roughly 9% over the past decade, mainstream mutual fund returns – averaged across the 7000 plus that exist – was roughly 6%, while the average mutual fund *investor* saw returns of only 3%.

Research has shown that the passive asset class investor – aided by a qualified adviser – stands to gain an additional two to three percentage points. Keeping in mind that *Dimensional* only works with a select group of fee-only advisers, (who may charge a percentage of assets under management), the adviser fee begins to look more like a sound investment. Who would not spend one dollar to make two – or even three?

In his book, *Winning the Loser's Game*, Charles Ellis points to research that shows investors tend to sabotage their own investments by hunting hot stocks or popular mutual funds. To level the playing field, Ellis has a few rules for capturing the returns of the market:

- Don't trust your emotions.
- Put your investment program and your financial goals in writing, and stick to them.
- Limit the amount you invest – don't bet the farm.
- Don't do anything that is primarily for tax reasons.
- Don't assume your financial adviser has your best interests in mind.
- Never invest in commodities.
- Beware of new or "interesting" investments.[59]

Mr. Ellis' list is an *anatomy of discipline*. The key points are that you need to establish your long-term investment objectives in writing and – with the expert advice of professionals – determine a well-reasoned and realistic investment plan that can help you achieve your objectives. You should set your asset mix at the highest ratio of equities you can afford financially and emotionally for the long-term.

However you do this, don't try to beat the market. That's the loser's game. Ellis emphasizes the importance of not making mistakes, not losing money relative to the market, staying in the market, and realizing that your real problem is beating inflation rather than the market. In general, doing less will be doing more. Avoid speculation, shifting funds continuously, and paying too much attention to near-term performance.

The role of the adviser in this context, what Ellis calls "the winner's game," will be to strengthen the resolve of the individual investor – so he or she will not break away from a diversified buy-in to the market, or fall back into the delusion of having found the secret bullet for beating the market.

The investment adviser plays the winner's game by finding out where the investor wants to go, and then accessing the capital markets to get him there. It is helpful to think of this relationship along the lines of the passenger, the pilot and the plane. Once you understand the enduring gains of the market, once you trust the mechanics of the plane, you are ready to begin the journey.

But imagine this scenario: No sooner are you aloft and cruising then along comes turbulence the like of which you've never seen before. What do you do? Until you experience the turbulence first hand, you cannot know how you would respond. The adviser – the pilot – on the other hand, has made the trip countless times, and the turbulence for him has become routine. The turbulence comes in the form of market fluctuations, and it is the adviser's task to prepare the investor for these harrowing moments, to see that they cause neither nausea nor a desire to abort the journey.

The most important variable is also the one you *can* control

Why do Tiger Woods, Andre Aggasi, Muhammed Ali, Michael Jordan, and hundreds of other sports legends have numerous personal trainers and coaches? Was it for lack of talent, or because of the absence of potential to excel without their coaches? Of course not. It was because these stars know the value of having someone there to keep them focused on the fundamentals. The upshot is more consistent winning.

Star athletes realize the benefit of having someone who can objectively help keep them focused during tough times, someone who will encourage them to do the *right* things, not the *easy* things. We also see this same attitude toward winning at work every day in the lives of top CEO's, who realize the benefit of having financial advisers and consultants assist and guide them. It is not that they don't have the potential within themselves to go it alone, it is rather that they understand the real-life benefit of having their own personal coach and adviser to help them stay focused on what they need to be, and keep them from hurting themselves with their own emotionalism.

We have examined how you can capture the returns of the markets via generic index funds or, better yet, when possible, institutional asset class funds. In spite of these opportunities, most investors, both individual and institutional, still end up being beaten by the market. Why does this muddled losers approach seem so intractable? The answer is easy to understand but difficult to concede. This is because the biggest obstacle to realizing investment success is yourself, or, more specifically, your behavior, particularly when motivated by the two emotional driving forces of the active investor: Fear and greed.

Market run-ups activate greed; the downturns spawn fear. It has always been this way, and it always will. Look back over the last 10 years, and you will find both emotions at work. The late 90's and up until early 2000 was greed's era. Phrases like "the new economy" were everywhere and, thanks to online access, investors were able to play financial roulette with their life savings for only $9.99 a bullet! One popular TV commercial showed a soccer mom sitting in front of her computer trading stocks while her neighbor looked on with envy. She assured her friend that buying and selling stocks online was easy and fun.

It was supposed to last for decades. Then suddenly, the "new economy" ran out of helium. No one likes to pay for yesterday's party. The bursting of the stock market bubble was followed by a recession, and the beginning of one of the sharpest, longest bear markets in history, lasting well over two years. Some stock indices were down well in excess of 60-70%. The party ended early, and many awoke to find they drank too much, and were now faced with a debilitating hangover. Pain morphed into resigned disappointment, only to fester and devolve into fear, intense fear, on the verge of panic. This final psychological phase is best described as the "get me out at any price syndrome."

Now look back at the last 200 years of financial markets – you find that the only way an investor would have realized a loss, assuming he owned most or all of the companies comprising a broad index, was to have sold during one of the temporary declines. Investors do it to themselves. Again, this is a recurring cycle of costly yet predictable behavior.

What makes people sell during temporary declines? They either need unexpected capital or they are victimized by their own fear. In the first case, investors often do not realize that capital can be made available without exiting the market – by turning to bonds, money markets or CD's, for instance. In the case of emotionalism, what is of primary importance is protection from oneself. In both instances what the losing player lacks is a "financial coach": Someone who can be there when you are most in need.

Hiring the right Financial Adviser (Coach) Is crucial to your financial future

As the world's successful athletes and CEO's reap the rewards of sound guidance and wisdom, most individuals and institutions who have achieved respectable and successful financial results have done so with the help of their own financial coach. They also have several strong beliefs in common, which include:

1. If left to their own devices, their own emotions will lead them to make many costly, destructive mistakes.

2. Hiring a financial coach who will contractually agree to legally serve as a fiduciary for them and their family is not an expense but rather one of the wisest investments they will ever make.

3. Having a comprehensive, written financial plan that serves as the roadmap for all of their future financial plans isn't just a good idea, it's financial wisdom at its best.

4. At the end of the day, it isn't investment returns that matter; it is rather real-life *investor returns* that count. And these returns are ultimately determined not by the financial markets as such but by the investors behavior. Fortunately, with the assistance of an experienced financial coach this variable is the one you can control.

Summing up

It is amazing how individuals and families will pay several thousands of dollars for a week's vacation but won't think of investing half as much to prepare for the longest vacation of their lives – retirement.

Commit to being a wise investor and not a speculator. Don't let the "hype" tempt you into making poor financial decisions. Use the following *Checklist for Interviewing Any Financial Adviser*, and begin your search for your own "financial coach" who will represent *your* interests and not those of Wall Street. Then you too can become a sleep-well-at-night investor.

The Essential Checklist
for Interviewing Any Financial Adviser

1. Compensation
- ✓ Do choose a Fee-Only adviser
- ✓ Don't use a Fee "Based" or Commission adviser
- ✓ Don't work with any adviser who holds *any* NASD licenses

2. Experience & Philosophy
- ✓ Do choose an adviser with at least 10 years experience
- ✓ Don't choose an adviser unless he/she is enrolled in continuing financial education
- ✓ Don't work with anyone who tries to time the market
- ✓ Do find out what will trigger changes in your portfolio
- ✓ Do find out about the sources of the adviser's research
- ✓ Do insist on an agreement that says your adviser accepts a fiduciary responsibility to invest in your best interest

3. Services Provided
- ✓ Do ask whether the adviser offers specific tax managed strategies
- ✓ Do insist on *annual* performance reports
- ✓ Do insist on a comprehensive written financial plan *before* you invest

4. Products Used
- ✓ Do make sure there are no commissions, or loads, attached to any products
- ✓ Do insist on *Passive* Management (i.e., index funds, etc.) rather than *Active* Management

2

A *Who's Who* of Mutual Fund Critics

Mutual fund criticism had gone largely ignored until the scandals of 2003 and 2004. The following is a selected list of critics that spans a five decade long tradition; it includes industry leaders, advisers, writers, investors, academics and Nobel Prize winners – all of whom go very much against the grain of the Wall Street status quo.

John Bogle

John Bogle started the first retail index fund, the Vanguard 500, in 1976. The best general introduction to Bogle's views is, *John Bogle on Investing: The First 50 Years* (Wiley & Sons, 2001). With a foreword by Paul Volker, the book is an outstanding collection of Bogle's speeches and presentations over the course of his career.

Bogle's latest book is really the bible of mutual fund criticism: *Common Sense on Mutual Funds: New Imperatives for the Intelligent Investor* (Wiley & Sons, 1999). For a decent biography, see: Robert Slater, *The Vanguard Experiment: John Bogle's Quest to Transform the Mutual Fund Industry* (1996).

Warren Buffett

Buffett has repeatedly criticized the financial industry for what he considers to be a proliferation of advisers who add no value but are compensated based on the volume of business transactions they facilitate. He has pointed to the growing volume of stock trades as evidence that an ever-greater proportion of investors' gains are going to brokers and other middle-men.

Mr. Buffett has amassed an enormous fortune from astute investments, particularly through the company Berkshire Hathaway, of which he is the largest shareholder and CEO. With an estimated current net worth of around $46 billion, he is ranked by Forbes as the second-richest person in the world.

Eugene Fama

Professor Fama is among the most prolific and cited thinkers in finance today. The author of two books and numerous articles, he focuses much of his study on market prices and implications for portfolio management. He is also an advisery editor of the Journal of Financial Economics and a fellow of the Econometric Society in the American Academy of Arts and Sciences. Awarded the Chaire Francqui (Belgian National Science Prize) in 1982, Professor Fama was also granted honorary law degrees by the University of Rochester and DePaul University.

The Robert R. McCormick Distinguished Service Professor of Finance at the Graduate School of Business at the University of Chicago, Professor Fama received his Ph.D. degree from the University of Chicago in 1964.

Kenneth R. French

Kenneth R. French is the Carl E. and Catherine M. Heidt Professor of Finance at the Tuck School of Business at Dartmouth College. He is an expert on the behavior of security prices and investment strategies. He and co-author Eugene F. Fama are well known for their research into the value effect and the three-factor model, including articles such as "The Cross-Section of Expected Stock Returns" and "Common Risk Factors in the Returns on Stocks and Bonds." His recent research focuses on tests of asset pricing, the tradeoff between risk and return in domestic and international financial markets, and the relation between capital structure and firm value.

Professor French is a research associate at the National Bureau of Economic Research, an advisery editor of the Journal of Financial Economics, a former associate editor of the Journal of Finance and the Review of Financial Studies, and a past director of the American Finance Association.

David & Tom Gardner

Founders of The Motley Fool, the Gardner's first book, *The Motley Fool Investment Guide* (Simon & Schuster, 1996), brought mutual fund criticism to a huge audience. Their site, www.fool.com, features a range of well-written critiques of the current state of affairs in the mutual fund industry. Though their site has recently become more product oriented, the book, and Tom Gardner's early articles on mutual funds remain classics.

Arthur Levitt

The speeches and presentations that Levitt gave as Chairman of the SEC are insightful and eloquent. They are all recommended highly and without qualification. You can find them on the SEC Web site: www.sec.gov. Go to news/speeches.

Harry M. Markowitz

Markowitz is the father of modern portfolio theory. His Nobel Prize winning work penetrates the evolution of the concepts of diversification and portfolio selection, with insight for today's investor.

Robert C. Merton

Dr. Merton's academic contributions, for which he won a Nobel Prize, ushered in the development of derivatives and systematic approaches to risk management.

Mary Rowland

Ms. Rowland's, *The New Common Sense Guide to Mutual Funds* (Bloomberg, 2000) was endorsed by Bogle as, "A splendid combination of wisdom and simplicity. The Dos and Don'ts offer a priceless education in what investors really need to know." (There are thirty-seven in all.) Ms. Rowland's online column for *Microsoft Investor* is also worth examining.

Paul A. Samuelson

Nobel Prize winner Paul A. Samuelson's application of mathematics to economic theory influenced finance and nearly every other field of modern economics.

William F. Sharpe

Dr. Sharpe's pioneering research into the relationship between risk and expected return forged a template for the entire discipline of asset pricing. His Nobel Prize winning ideas provide much of the basis for modern investing thinking.

Larry Swedroe

In *What Wall Street Doesn't Want You to Know* (St. Martins, 2001) Swedroe debunks many of the myths perpetuated by the financial media. His frontal assault against actively managed mutual funds is comprehensive and persuasive. He has written numerous in-depth articles against active money management for www.indexfunds.com. Swedroe is the Director of Research for Buckingham Asset Management and BAM Advisor Services.

Jim Wiandt & Will McClatchy

Co-editors of www.indexfunds.com, these journalists are passive investing purists. Their site offers information for everyone from the beginner to the academic. They have written many articles together, connecting academic proof against actively managed mutual funds with mainstream media myths and public perception.

Their book, *Exchange Traded Funds: An Insider's Guide to Buying the Market* (Wiley & Sons, 2001), is the most lucid and comprehensive introduction to the new investment vehicle otherwise known as ETFs. ETFs are also featured on their Web site.

Steve Wallman

Wallman is a former commissioner of the SEC. He was widely recognized during his tenure for advocacy efforts on behalf of individual investors. Wallman is the founder of www.foliofn.com, a Web site that provides self-directed portfolio investing.

This site is the culmination of Wallman's diagnosis of the mutual fund industry. In addition to providing an alternative way to invest, the site has numerous articles on the shortcomings of mutual funds.

ENDNOTES

[1] Robert J. Shiller, *Irrational Exuberance*, Princeton University Press, 2003.

[2] John Bogle, *Not-So Mutual Funds*, Mar 15, 2006, *The Wall Street Journal*, November 14, 2003.

[3] Books and studies that show the impossibility of beating the market over the long term include B. Millikan's excellent work, *A Random walk Down Wall Street (2007, ninth edition)*, Nobel Laureate Ben Johnson's work , *Efficient Market Theory* (1986), Harvard economist and investment adviser Charles Ellis' classic, *The Loser's Game* and Yale Economist's William Schiller's best seller, *Irrational Exuberance* (2002). The most articulate populizer of these ideas is John Bogle, whose latest book is, *The Little Book of Common Sense Investing,* (2007).

[4] Remarks by John C. Bogle, The Miller Center of Public Affairs, The University of Virginia, Charlottesville, VA, February 8, 2006.

[5] Ibid.

[6] Charles Ellis, *The Winner's Game*, *The Journal of Portfolio Management*, Spring, 2005.

[7] loma.org/retirementconference.asp

[8] Dustin Woodward, *Mutual Fund Mergers*, http://mutualfunds.about.com/od/news/a/fund_mergers.htm

[9] John Bogle, *Mutual Funds and Taxes*, An unpublished Letter to the Wall Street Journal, April 12, 2006,

http://johncbogle.com/wordpress/2006/04/12/mutual-funds-and-taxes/

[10] *Investment Company Act of 1940*,
http://www.bowne.com/pdf0307/invact40.pdf.

[11] *Annual Report, Berkshire Hathaway*, 1996.

[12] John Bogle. *Common Sense on Mutual Funds.* p. 190.

[13] Santoli, Michael. "Polished Performance." Barron's, December 11, 2006.

[14] Michael Mulvihill, *A Question of Trust*, Morningstar Mutual Funds,30 August, 1996. pp S1-S2.

[15] Paul Roye. *Navigating the Mutual Fund Industry through Challenging Times*,
http://www.sec.gov/news/speech/spch491.htm.

[16] New York Times, *In Good Times or Bad, Funds Offer Managers Rich Lures.*
http://www.iceved.com/ICEVED3/Servicio.nsf/17d0294935b6b
bb7412568b80039b54f/b2c0209f98ca2d9741256a8b0055c419?
OpenDocument

[17] John Bogle's keynote speech at the National Investment Company Service Association's 2007 Conference. See MutualFundScandalWatch.com, Archive May 5, 2007.

[18] John Bogle. *Common Sense on Mutual Funds.* p 19.

[19] Paul Roye. The Exciting World of Investment Company Regulation.
http://www.sec.gov/news/speech/spch500.htm

[20] Ms. Richards made these remarks over the telephone, and granted permission for their reproduction here.

[21] Margaret Myers, *Information Disclosure Regulation and the Returns to Active Management in the Mutual Fund Industry.* http://econ-
   www.mit.edu/faculty/poterba/files/copycatoct2001.pdf.

[22] Larry Swedrowe, What Wall Street Doesn't Want You to Know: How You can Profit from the Indexing Revolution, St. Martins, 2001.

[23] *Redemptions of Mutual Fund Investors, Fundamentals,* Investment Company Institute, Vol. 10 Number 1, 2001.

[24] *Fidelity and Janus Added Loaded Funds*, Morningstar, June, 2007. http://news.morningstar.com/article/article.asp?id=180693&pgid
=wwhome1a

[25] Will McClatchy, *Fidelity Giants' Holdings Mirror Vanguard.* http://www.indexfunds.com/PFarticles/*20000821*_fidelity_iss_ac
   t_WM.htm

[26] Mary Rowland, *The New Common Sense Guide to Mutual Funds*, Bloomberg Press. 1998. p 26.

[27] Mary Rowland. *The New Common Sense Guide to Mutual Funds*. p 70.

[28] Larry Swedroe, *Survivorship Bias.* www.indexfunds.com/articles/20010143_survivorship_com_act_
LS.htm

[29] *ibid*, p.119.

[30] In theory, funds may also be able to achieve better performance by doing these mergers as a result of cost savings. For example, funds pay by the trust series to be listed on platforms such as Schwab, Fidelity, etc. They also may pay their

transfer agencies a flat fee for each fund, pay additional marketing expenses for each fund, etc. These cost savings may, theoretically, result in better returns for investors.

[31] Arthur Levitt, *The Future for America's Investors – Their Rights and Obligations*, Investors' Town Hall Meeting. January, 2001. http://www.sec.gov/news/speech/spch457.htm.

[32] Survival of the fittest fund, MarketWatch, April, 2007.

[33] *SEC News Digest*, Commission Announcements. September 2000.
http://198.252.9.108/govper/SECNews/www.sec.gov/news/digests/2000/09/0925.txt

[34] http://www.sec.gov/litigation/admin/34-43215.htm

[35] *New York Times*. November 21, 2001.

[36] John Bogle, *Bogle Financial Markets Research Center*. March 2001.
http://www.vanguard.com/bogle_site/march212001.html

[37] Arthur Levitt, *Mutual Fund Directors' Education Council Conference*. http://www.sec.gov/news/speech/spch346.htm

[38] *Boone Advisers*,
http://www.booneadvisers.com/ourviews/articles/07152001_172827.shtml

[39] *Mutual Fund Fees May be too High,* Detroit News. July 2000.
http://www.detnews.com/2000/business/0007/23/c01-94361.htm

[40] Will McClatchy & Jim Wiandt., *A Study on Waste.*
http://www.indexfunds.com/articles/20001010_wastestudy2_adv_act_WMJW.ht

[41] Tom Gardner, *Testimony to U.S. Congress*. http://www.the fool.com/mutualfunds/gardner/

[42] *High time for fund-fee review, says SEC's Cox*, Market Watch, April, 2007.

[43] Arthur Levitt, *The Future for America's Investors–Their Rights and Obligations*, Investors' Town Hall Meeting. January, 2001. http://www.sec.gov/news/speech/spch457.htm.

[44] *SEC Press Release*. January, 2001. http://www.sec.gov/news/press/2001-2.txt

[45] *SEC Press Release*. January, 2001. http://www.sec.gov/news/press/2001-2.txt

[46] *A Raw Deal for Fund Shareholders*, Business Week. July 2000. http://www.businessweek.com/2000/00_31/b3692103.htm

[47] A Conflict of Interest, *Financial Planning Interactive*. January 2000.

[48] See Hugh Bullock, *The Story of Investment Companies*. New York, Columbia University Press. 1959.

[49] Time, Vol. LXXIII, No. 22. June 1, 1959.

[50] Ibid.

[51] Ibid.

[52] John Bogle. *Common Sense on Mutual Funds.* p. 293 ff.

[53] Ibid. p. 294.

116

[54] M. Rowland. op cit. p 237.

[55] Larry Swedroe, *The Road Less Traveled*, November 2001.
http://www.indexfunds.com/PFarticles/20011114_road_iss_act_
LS.htm

[56] James Garland, *The Attraction of Tax-Managed Index Funds*,
The Journal of Investing. Vol. 6. Spring 1997. p. 13-20.

[57] J. Bogle, *As The Index Fund Moves from Heresy to Dogma . . .
What More Do We Need To Know?* The Gary M. Brinson
Distinguished Lecture, Bogle Financial Center, (2004-04-13).

[58] J. Bogle. op cit. p. 348.

[59] Charles D. Ellis, author of *Winning the Loser's Game*,
(McGraw-Hill; 2002).